BUSINESS TIPS

from the

How to Succeed
in Business
Without an MBA

45 "BIG LESSONS"
They Don't Teach You in College

by Chuck Trautman

Business Tips from the Trenches
How to Succeed in Business Without an MBA

Cover design and layout by Hollister Design Group

Photography by Rick Mueller Photography

Published by 23 Kazoos LLC

ISBN # 978-0-9844034-4-8

"I've had the good fortune to know Chuck Trautman for several years. We've been in a Mastermind group together and I've been very impressed with his depth and breadth of real-world business experience. The true business stories he uses in this book are not only instructive, but entertaining as well. You're guaranteed to get some great value and more than a few smiles when you read it."

> ~ Henry Evans
> Author of *The Hour a Day Entrepreneur*
> Founder of the Hour A Day Entrepreneur Academy

"I wanted to take a moment and let you know that the Mastermind session we just had in Napa Valley was by far the best Mastermind I've attended in my years as an entrepreneur. You did a marvelous job choosing the venue, creating an environment where the group can share and being an excellent facilitator. I'm looking forward to the next one. Anyone who is serious about taking their business to the next level should attend!"

> ~ Richard James Strauch
> CEO, Automated Business Results, LLC

"Chuck runs a tight meeting, full of content and with a sincere desire to help the members grow their businesses. Great participation from other members – all of who are just not learning but doing."

> ~ Bill Cantrell
> OnPoint Financial Strategies, LLC

"Chuck is a shining example of Napoleon Hill's teaching re: enthusiasm. I leave with his energetic example after each session."

> ~ Steve Rensch
> Rensch Law

"Chuck is so real! He's been super successful himself and genuinely wants to help other marketers be successful."

> ~ Norm Jones
> Site Cipher

"Chuck, great job last night. Gave me some organization around the multiple freight trains buzzing around in my head, as well as some new additions to the mix."

> ~ Jim Hart
> Direct Marketing Consultant

"Awesome ideas we can take and use in our business right away! I got more from one monthly meeting than I have from entire seminars in the past. Thanks, Chuck!"

> ~ Nick Trevillain
> Go Sold Realty

"If you are a struggling business owner, I don't fell sorry for you! You have to come to Chuck's mastermind meeting once a month. The strategies that are gone over are priceless. So quit reading and get to Chuck's mastermind so you can witness how many businesses are changing overnight."

> ~ Phil Shaver
> Go Sold Realty

"Every time I come, I learn something fantastic. The other members are all high caliber business people. I am honored to be associated with Chuck and his organization."

> ~ Nancy Smith
> Alliance Financial Resources

"Chuck is the perfect leader and one of the reasons I come to monthly meetings. Chuck is very supportive and giving to group meetings."

> ~ Dr. Tara Revell
> Anthem, AZ

"Chuck, thanks for showing what a leader does. The big 'aha' is your attitude. Technical and marketing skills are all important, but without the right attitude, it's all for naught. Thanks for all you do."

> ~ Mike Weiss

DEDICATION

This book is dedicated to my wife, Carol, who's had my back my entire adult life; my two daughters, Tara and Amy, for whom I've tried to set a good example; and my four grandchildren, Gretta, Ellie, Tyler, and Reese – works in progress whom I love to see grow as people.

Business Tips From the Trenches is dedicated to US Military Veterans whom have given so much for our great country. Without the sacrifices of veterans going back to colonial days there never would have been a society where entrepreneurs can flourish. It is my hope that many veterans find inspiration from this book and launch their own entrepreneurial journeys.

And finally this book is dedicated to entrepreneurs everywhere who have the guts to keep the world economy progressing in spite of the ignorance of government officials who don't understand our independent spirits.

Carol and I with our grandkids, Gretta, Ellie, Tyler and Reese.

TABLE OF CONTENTS

INTRODUCTION

My mentor, Dan Kennedy, says to always tell your back story so here is mine. This is not an attempt to write an autobiography. This is a book of true stories where I relate life experiences with lessons for business and life success which I put in boxes after each story called (Big Lessons).

To answer the "What's In It For Me" question from my readers is that the lessons were learned from living a life in the trenches. If you want to get through this book quickly, flip pages to the " ★ **BIG LESSONS**." If the lesson resonates with you, read the story that precedes it.

CHAPTER 1

Growing Up

I was born in Portland, Oregon. I endured a major life-changing event when my father passed away when I was just 13 years old and in the 7th grade. Until then it was all about being absorbed in sports and getting high marks in school, because Dad took care of everything else.

Between 8th and 9th grade, my mother made the decision for us to spend the summer in Ellensburg, WA where her mother, step-father, and two sisters lived. They had six acres with a pond on it. I helped my grandfather, whom I idolized, with the chores and he taught me how to fish for bass, shoot, and do all sorts of handyman repairs. I loved that summer, but I missed playing baseball with my Pony League team which went on to win the Oregon State Championship without me, their leading hitter!

My grandfather died during my 9th grade year. He had been sick for years so it was not unexpected. After struggling in Portland for three years, my mother moved us to Ellensburg, WA that summer. In those days in Oregon you could get a driver learner's permit when you were 15. I point this out because it started my love affair with cars.

We moved ourselves. Picture this: a 15 year old kid driving a Nash Rambler pulling a 5' x 12' U-Haul trailer making three, 450 mile round trips in five days on mostly two-lane roads with his mother asleep most of the time because she was dog tired!

> ★ **BIG LESSON**
>
> You do what you have to do. The human mind and body are strong and you can will yourself through anything.

That summer I got my first job outside of paper routes and berry picking in Portland. Another kid and I were hired by a farmer to "shock oats." The farmer, Eldon Bird, did not have a combine so shocking oats consisted of standing up the straw in 3 shock triangles so the grain would dry in the sun. He was afraid to pay us by the hour because he thought we would be slow so he paid us $100 each to work 17 acres.

I must have been an OK worker for him because he hired me to pitch fork the dried shocks into his threshing machine and later to buck hay bales behind his baler and then to pick them up and stack them in his barn. By the time football practice started I was a pretty strong kid.

Over the next few summers I was "in demand" by many local farmers. I've bucked hay, plowed fields, built fence, irrigated, built loafing sheds and barns, and even branded, castrated and de-horned cattle.

Somewhere in there I bought a goat, had it bred, and raised her "kids" (baby goats). The purpose was to use their milk to feed bum lambs. I could buy them for $2 (bum lambs are lambs turned away by their mother or orphaned). Eventually, while my buddies were milking a cow or two by hand, I was milking three goats twice-a-day and my mom and I bottle fed lambs. Then we would either sell them for meat or raise them to adulthood and sell the wool.

> **★ BIG LESSON**
>
> The entrepreneur in me was born! I learned that with a plan and work ethic you could turn almost anything into money.

With the money from that enterprise I bought an old, white, gelding horse named Napoleon for $125. That was fun for a while, but I sold him to buy my first car, a 1946 GMC pickup. I like to joke that the driver in my golf bag cost more than my first two cars added together!

An ad in the local newspaper advertised a class to learn how to become a service station attendant. In those days service station attendants did more than pump gas. Lube jobs, fixing flat tires, wheel balancing, oil changes and other light mechanical skills were also required. I signed up because it would give me the opportunity to work somewhere part time during the school year.

The instructor was the owner of a busy Union 76 station in Ellensburg. The class was cancelled because of lack of registrations. I went to the station and told the owner that I would like to work Saturdays for free to learn the skills. After 3 weeks he hired me to work for pay – $1.25 an hour!

> **★ BIG LESSON**
>
> I always tell everyone the best way to get a job is to offer to work for free while you learn. The same thing goes for starting a new service business or launching a new info product. Take on a couple of clients for free, develop your skills, and then use the case studies of their success in your sales process.

The assistant manager of that station, Duane Medved, bought the Texaco station in town. He offered me $1.35 an hour and more hours to work for him. The summer after my senior year I worked 3:30 to 11:30 PM at Texaco and Midnight to 8 AM at the Union 76 station.

Somehow, with all this going on I still managed to play high school football and baseball, and become a motor head.

CHAPTER 2

The Car Days

My grandmother bought me a completely stock, 1928 Model A Ford 2-door sedan as a gift for working on her property. I drove it as a stock Model A, mechanical brakes and all for a while. But eventually the bug to build a hot rod got me. By this time, I had learned to buy old cars, fix them up, and sell them at a profit.

I put a 1948 Mercury differential and transmission in it, converted it to hydraulic brakes and clutch, and bought an adapter to convert the bell housing of a 1956, 292 C.I. (cubic inch) Ford V8 to the '48 Merc transmission. The father of a high school friend, Larry Schnebly, let me use his barn for the engine swap and Larry helped me with it.

When I first got it running I couldn't wait until it was really road ready. On its virgin run it had no floorboards and no gas pedal. I had a piece of baling wire attached to the carburetor and used it as a hand throttle. I took a girl I was attempting to date for a ride. I did not impress her with the dust and exhaust swirling up from where the floor should have been!

Before I was 21 I had bought and sold 20 cars and two motor-cycles. I had some beauties. To name a few not mentioned above, I had a 1930 Model A Ford Roadster with a 1957 Ford V8, a 1934 Ford pickup with a 1948 Mercury V8, a stock 1940 Ford Coupe, a 1955 Chevy Convertible, a 1957 Chevy 2-door Hardtop, a 1957 Ford Convertible with a souped up 312 V8, and a 1950 Chevy Business Coupe. Later on I had a couple of real fast Chevelles and 1956 Chevy Nomad.

The '50 Chevy Business Coupe was the fastest one of all. I put a 371 Pontiac V8 Tri-Power (three 2-barrel carburetors) and a GMC truck transmission and differential in it. I had it muffled down so the unsuspecting street racer thought it had the stock 6-cylinder engine in it. The car flew and I took many $5 and $10 bets off the naïve boys who thought their machines could beat mine.

1965 Chevelle, 327, 4 speed. "Trophied" with it at the Ellensburg, WA Drag Strip.

CHAPTER 3

The Lost Years

When I graduated from high school many of the "rich kids" got brand new cars for graduation gifts. I was not jealous or envious but it did make me think about wanting to make more money than what I was making. I never wanted for any necessity after my dad died, my mom saw to that, but we never enjoyed the "luxuries" either.

My grades were good in high school and I could play a little baseball. For that I earned a scholarship to what is now Central Washington State University. My heart was never in immediately going to college after high school, but I went anyway because of the scholarship and student draft status. I probably was burned out because I worked so much in addition to school. So I worked, partied hard, and only went to class when I felt like it. After two quarters they asked me to leave. This was not a good plan at the time.

I'm not hung up on the importance of college degrees for young men except for those wanting to go into medicine, law or some other field requiring special skills. I feel differently about young women. We made sure both of our daughters received their degrees. I also believe there should be a mandatory two-year service program for everyone to allow them to grow up.

My "flunk out" was during the Viet Nam War so I knew I would eventually get drafted into the Armed Forces. In the mean time I met this girl, now my long time best friend and wife, Carol. I decided to move to Seattle and go to work for Boeing to save some money before getting drafted. They were hiring for "big bucks" (for the times) for factory workers.

I was a tool fabricator working with fiberglass. What a shitty job! Being a riveter would have been worse, but I could not stand the tedium. I knew right then that I had to get my service hitch behind me and make something of myself because I did NOT want to work in a factory for a career.

★ **BIG LESSON**

Sometimes finding out what you don't want to do is a real asset and helps motivate you.

CHAPTER 4

The US Marine Years

I received my draft notice and went to see the Marine Corps recruiter. Prior to moving to Seattle I had tried to join the Air National Guard. They would not take me because my juvenile record disclosed four "serious offenses" of minor possessing and minor consuming alcohol. When I told the Marine recruiter about it he laughed and said, "In the Marines we see that as a sign of aggressiveness. Sign on the dotted line." I knew I had found a home.

After I enlisted in the Marines, my reporting date was 90 days out. I quit Boeing's immediately and worked full time as a farm hand for three months. It was for a lot less money, but was a helluva lot more satisfying work.

When I decided to join the Marines, my attitude was, "You can't draft me in the Army for two years, I'll show you – I'll enlist in the Marines for four years." It turns out it was a great decision. I grew up, learned much about myself, and found out I was a leader.

*1966 Carol and Chuck wedding picture –
note the "white sidewall" Marine haircut.*

Carol and I were married right after Marine boot camp. She's followed me around the world ever since. Obviously she has a ton of patience!

My test scores were very high so after boot camp they assigned me to an aviation school at the Naval Air Station in Millington, TN to become an aircraft mechanic. My MOS was 6341. Basically I was trained to work on the air conditioning and pressurization systems of all aircraft and the ejection seats of fighter and attack jets.

★ **BIG LESSON**

**Having brains and common sense is always an asset.
Then you plan to just "play dumb" when necessary.**

I graduated from aircraft maintenance school on Dec. 22nd with orders to Viet Nam. We had 30 days of leave before reporting for "staging" at Camp Pendleton in CA. Carol and I decided to "get home for Christmas." We loaded everything we had (not much) in our 1965 Chevelle and headed for Kennewick, WA, 2,300 miles away. Driving straight through we made it in 47 ½ hours. Of course I slept through most of Christmas.

My overseas assignment was to VMGR 152, a KC130 (the "K" designates an aerial refueling tanker) squadron based in Futema, Okinawa, so initially no Viet Nam duty to start.

Of course after getting some practical experience, I was sent to Da Nang for a 60-day maintenance detachment. Besides doing our own jobs we helped each other on the other aircraft systems (jet engine, hydraulics, avionics, etc.)

Here's a little war story for you. Occasionally we came under rocket attack. In these instances, as Marines, half of my unit went to the perimeter to defend against possible insurgents. Most of the defense was done by the real Marines (infantry), not we Marine Air boys.

Da Nang in 1966. Chuck in front of a Lockheed KC 130 Hercules.

After one such instance where we returned fire (you were just shooting at muzzle flash not people), it was discovered that some of the enemy dead were barbers from the Air Force PX. I had just had my hair cut that very day. It gave me a chill to think that one of those guys had trimmed my neck with a straight razor. Who the hell knows? I may have shot my barber!

★ **BIG LESSON**

Beware of complacency. It can be fatal in life and business.

It was then that I decided I wanted to be part of the flight crew. In the Air Force the six members of a C130 flight crew are all officers. In the Marine Corps only the pilot and co-pilot are officers. The rest of the crew is enlisted.

I asked a couple of staff sergeants who were flight engineers what I needed to learn to fly as a first mechanic. They gave me the list, expecting I would be overwhelmed, and give up. I fooled 'em by learning quickly and soon I was part of the flight crew rotation.

The rotation was to leave Okinawa and fly five hours to Da Nang with troops and cargo. We flew "in country" for four days hauling troops, supplies and jet fuel to Chu Lai, Dong Ha, Phu Bai, and Khe Sanh or flying aerial refueling missions. Then we'd return to Da Nang with troops, medevac's, Viet Cong POW's and bodies.

After four days we returned to Futema for a day of crew rest. The rotation was completed with what was called "augmentation crew." Essentially we flew to Da Nang for five days. We slept by day and at night we flew aerial refueling missions or dropped hundreds

My commanding officer at MARTD. Alameda pinning on my first Air Medal in 1968.

of million candlepower flares over active fire fights. Then we again returned to Okinawa for a day of crew rest.

I was awarded two Air Medals for this service. A small number compared to some of my buddies who were gunners on helicopters, but none the less, something I am proud of.

> ★ **BIG LESSON**
>
> By being willing to do more than what was asked of me, I got additional education and earned combat pay and flight pay every month. This has been my pattern throughout my life and I highly recommend it to those who aspire to be the best. Do more than the minimum required to "get by" and you'll never regret it.

Upon returning to the states, I saw the "wisdom" of the military first hand. Instead of being sent to one of the two active KC130 squadrons in the US where I could use my skills and advance my training as an air crewman, I was assigned to a Marine Air Reserve Training Detachment at the Naval Air Station in Alameda, CA.

My job for the last two years of my service was to train Marine Reserves to perform maintenance on A4 attack fighters. It was pretty much a thankless job. The reserves did not want to be there and only joined to keep from being drafted and the outfit itself was far more spit and polish than I was accustomed to.

One of our reserves was Dick Tidrow. If you're a baseball fan you recognize the name as he went on to play for the New York Yankees. At the time Dick was playing in the minors for the Reno Silver Sox. When his unit went to its mandatory two weeks of summer camp, I brought a catcher's mitt and Dick threw to me to keep up his arm strength.

At the time I had just made sergeant. I was sent out to supervise two reserves washing three A4s. I reasoned that if I only supervised the job it would take three hours because the reserves would milk the job, but if I pitched in it we would get done in 1 ½ hours. As we were finishing up, I was reprimanded by a master sergeant because "sergeants don't wash airplanes." I never understood that way of thinking. I know I gained the respect of the reserves, who would cheerfully do anything I asked in the future.

The fun stuff was the sports. We had unit teams in football, basketball, volleyball and fast pitch softball and the Naval Air Station had base teams that played football, basketball and baseball. I played on every team I could. The quality of competition was high (a lot of former college athletes played) and the hitting in football was a lot fiercer than I ever experienced in high school.

They were always begging for officials. The base recreation department paid $5 a game for intramural games. I attended a class for prospective umpires and was certified to umpire softball games on the base.

I was a good umpire so I was asked to call inter-base baseball games for $15 a game. Lil Arnerich, at the City of Alameda recreation department saw me call a game, and ask me to call two games a night for the Alameda City Adult League for $6 a game. That led to calling Babe Ruth Baseball for $7.50 a game. The baseball coach at St. Elizabeth HS in Oakland saw me call a Babe Ruth game and recommended me to call high school games for the Catholic Athletic League in Oakland for $22.50 a game. I would have tried to make professional umpiring a career but I wore glasses at the time!

I have no regrets about my four years in the Marine Corps. I learned a lot about myself, leadership and growing up. I am convinced those four years shaped me for who I am today.

★ **BIG LESSON**

As a married guy in the service, money was tight even though Carol worked full time at a bank. The umpiring gave us money to see a lot of things in the SF Bay Area and I enjoyed the hell out of it. Many people have worked two or more jobs at the same time. I don't understand an entitlement mentality.

CHAPTER 5

College?

When I was discharged from the Marines I stayed in California with the intent to go back to college. I worked for the City of Alameda as a recreation leader at the city parks and continued to officiate softball, baseball and basketball. Do you see what a little step to get ahead turned into? Part time income for a new dad in college was a big deal.

Because of my US Marine background, the city assigned me to parks where there were discipline problems with the kids. I imposed my will on the kids and their parents, sometimes doing things that would get me fired for sure and probably arrested in today's world (nothing serious, just a slap on the face or a push against a wall). But after a rough start the kids and parents loved me for my leadership and respected the discipline I injected into their lives.

At the Alameda City parks the recreation directors coached the youth teams in the city league. My teams were always good because they were shaped to play with heart and discipline. A couple of my kids on my teams had dads who were

Alameda City Police Officers. They tried to recruit me to join the police force, but I didn't see myself as a cop either.

I enrolled in Laney Community College in Oakland. I had talked to the baseball coach about playing and had attended a few practices. He approached me at practice one afternoon and said he was sorry but I wasn't eligible. The reason was that my parents did not live in the Laney Community College district. He agreed that it was pretty absurd to require that from a 24 year old, former Marine sergeant Viet Nam vet, but his hands were tied. I had expected to catch for Central Wash. St six years earlier and now this. I was pissed because my college baseball career was over before I ever played in a game!

I had witnessed government and military stupidity during my four years in the Marines and now from the State of California. I have had a low opinion of all government operations ever since. There have been several events in my business life that continue to reinforce that opinion.

School was boring and a waste of time. My GPA was 3.8 so I proved I could excel in school. However 24 year old, former Marine Sergeant Viet Nam vets, were not readily accepted by anti-war students and faculty in that era which led to some internal conflicts.

CHAPTER 6

Corporate America

With a wife and a new baby, I decided to look for a corporate job. I was hired by the Gates Rubber Company as an Automotive Dealer Salesman to cover the Oakland, Stockton, Modesto California area. I was given two weeks of thorough training, a company car and a very small expense account. I called on service stations, garages, and truck fleets. It was a "trade service work for sales" kind of job. I made quota every week my first year.

Gates was big in hydraulic hose and couplings in the industrial market but small potatoes in the automotive division. They started an automotive hydraulic specialist program but my zone was not selected to participate. I lobbied my immediate boss who told me to forget about it so I lobbied his boss about the position.

The head of the program, John Riess, interviewed me, and ask me to write a report on why my region should have a specialist. That was pretty easy since the region included San Francisco, Oakland, San Jose, Sacramento, Portland and Seattle. Those cities were home to some of the largest truck fleets in the country who were prime prospects for our products.

I was promoted to Fleet Hydraulic Specialist and sent to Rockford, IL in January for 2 weeks of training. I aced the class and learned an appreciation for the hardy souls who live on flat land where it is below zero with at least a 20 MPH wind blowing the entire time.

> ★ **BIG LESSON**
>
> **You never get what you desire if you don't ask for it. If you'd love to have something, use self-promotion and ask for it.**

For the next 1 ½ years I traveled the western states selling millions of feet of hydraulic hose. It was pretty easy. I led with Gates Green Strip fleet products where Gates was the industry leader and then convinced fleets to buy hydraulic hose because Gates was also a prime manufacturer.

Then I was promoted to District Sales Manager for Oregon and then to Zone Sales Manager for Oregon, SW Washington and Southern Idaho. I was successful, made many great friends and have some great stories to tell. But I also learned that corporate jobs always frustrate true entrepreneurs.

During the first big gas crunch in 1973, we waited in lines for hours to buy 10 gallons of gas. Gas theft ran rampant so locking gas caps were in huge demand. Gates sold locking gas caps and I booked orders for $450,000 worth of them. Had they been able to ship them, I'd have made an extra $13,500 in commission. Gates was outsourcing their gas caps from a manufacturer who was supplying their own distribution channels first so they were very slow in supplying their private label customers with locking gas caps.

The #2 man in the Gates automotive division called on my 2nd largest customer with me. He promised my customer they would have $100,000 worth of locking gas caps in a week. My customer said any time he needed something he would call John because I obviously could not get stuff done.

Of course the caps were never delivered. It was not possible. The corporate brass just made himself out to be a hero. When my customer called him to ask where the caps were, he denied making the promise – and I was there and I heard him make it. Since he was the big boss, I was told to keep my mouth shut.

Later, my immediate boss agreed to sell a new distributor in Eugene, OR, headquarters of my largest customer. He did this against my advice. Then when he heard we would lose half the business from our largest customer, he instructed me to meet with the new distributor and tell them Gates would not sell them. They were really pissed but did understand that I was only the messenger and that my boss had no courage.

Ah the corporate life – so glad I was out it at age 30.

CHAPTER 7

The Auto Parts Business

Soon after that my largest customer, Pacific Wholesalers, approached me about buying an auto parts store in Eugene. I said I'd love to but didn't have any money. They said they liked my work ethic and intelligence and for a $5,000 investment, would give me 10 percent of the store, assume the bank financing, and allow me to buy them out over time. It was too good an opportunity to pass up, so Carol, our daughter and 2nd daughter on the way moved from Vancouver, WA to Eugene, OR to buy Harr Motor Supply.

The man who owned Pacific Wholesalers was Lou Southworth. Lou was a quiet man who looked for ways to give opportunity to others. He wanted to keep it discreet about being involved in owning the majority of an auto parts store, because his other customers might have called "foul" in those days. Lou let me run the store as if I owned 100 percent of it.

Lou passed away several years ago, but we're still close friends with Lou's oldest daughter, Vicki and his son-in-law and best friend Dick Harrington.

Harr Motor Supply had a solid reputation but was not aggressive at all. I brought a lot of fire to the business and quickly turned it into a dynamo. The store had never done more than $31,000 in sales in a month (1976 dollars). By the end of the first year, I had it to $50,000 a month and had tripled the sales and profits by the end of the 2nd year.

As a partnership we bought Buy Right Auto Parts in Stayton, OR. By adding "fire" I doubled that business in a year.

Knowing I was "the man," we bought a rundown store in Salem, OR. Boy did we get our ass kicked. We could slay 'em with a sale, but we could not get 'em to come back and be an everyday, regular customer.

> ★ **BIG LESSON**
>
> Keep your ego in check. Whenever you think you know everything, the universe kicks your ass.

Back at Harr Motor Supply we were in a pinch to supply the import car market. Most of the American aftermarket manufacturers did a poor job of supplying parts for imported cars. Maremont Corp had its World Parts division which offered mediocre coverage at high prices.

I decided I had to do something. We were the market leader in Eugene for domestic car parts but the import car specialty stores, Beck Arnley and BAP Geon, were doing a number on us on imported car parts.

On the east coast, Vera Imported Parts rivaled Beck Arnley and BAP Geon. I contacted Vera and became their first West Coast outlet. We built a separate import car parts department with a separate counter and an "import car parts specialist" manning the counter. We had a huge sales jump from it.

Interesting Fact: The cars didn't know if they were "foreign" or "domestic" – only the owner knew. Perception was the key.

Lou Southworth watched our success and knew that the 100 auto parts stores he supplied in SW Washington, Oregon and Northern California could benefit from my program. He asked me to work with Vera on his behalf to put together their first wholesale program for domestic warehouse distributors.

In December of 1980, Lou and I flew to New York and met with Vera at their headquarters in Piscataway, NJ. I'll never forget the date because John Lennon was shot at his New York apartment the first night we were there.

We "made a deal" with Vera. Now Lou and Pacific Wholesalers needed someone to implement their new import parts program. Lou offered to exchange my stock in Charles F Trautman, Inc, the company that owned our auto parts stores, for stock in Pacific Wholesalers with the caveat that I had the option to do a reverse exchange later if I wished. So I became the VP of Special Markets for this $12 million a year auto parts distribution company. Although I loved my stores I saw this as an opportunity to eventually purchase the larger company.

I never looked at the Pacific financial statements because I idolized Lou and never suspected they had financial problems. That was a huge mistake, as you'll see later.

★ BIG LESSON

When buying or selling a business you have to know the numbers. Do not rely on friendship or reputation alone.

In the next couple of months I put together the marketing plan for what would be the largest product launch the auto parts industry had ever seen in the Northwest and maybe nationally. We rolled out the program with dinner meetings in Bend, Medford, Eugene and Portland, Oregon. The strategy was to start in the smallest market and perfect our pitch on the fly. By the 4th night I was exhausted from the stress, but somehow willed myself to almost perfection from the stage in Portland.

Propelled by those presentations we sold over $700,000 worth of Vera Imported Parts in the first 60 days of the launch. I was on the road with the salesmen calling on their largest accounts.

I was in Longview, WA on a Thursday, where I had just closed another $25,000 sale. Lou called and said I had to be in Eugene for a corporate officers meeting with the bank at 9 AM on Friday. I explained that I was on a roll and didn't have time for such bullshit and I was sure the other corporate officers would be fine without me since I was the newest officer. Lou explained to me that my attendance wasn't optional it was required.

The next day, the banker, Ray Sprung, of First National Bank of Boston, explained to us that he had been trying to tell Lou and our comptroller, Mack Albretson, that we were in deep trouble and were in danger of losing our financing. He explained the situation by saying this is like a football game, it's the 2-minute warning, you're down 10 points and you don't have the ball! What an analogy.

I was absolutely shocked, because I knew I had sold $700,000 of new business in 60 days. We should have been rolling in cash.

In hind sight I guess I was pretty naïve because we were still in the Jimmy Carter recession, the logging industry which drove the northwest economy at the time was dying, and the stores Pacific served were also struggling. My stores had not experienced the recession because I would not allow it. We just captured greater market share by going after it. It was that old mind over matter thing again.

The next day the team met. Lou moved up to chairman of the board, appointed Chris Winters, a long time sales manager at Pacific who would later become my partner, as President and me as Executive VP and head hatchet man. The comptroller was demoted.

The next two years were a blur. Chris and I cut $528,000 of annual expense (fat) out of a $12 million company. We laid

Chuck and Chris Winters on the cover of Automotive News

off 22 employees the first week and productivity went up. The layoffs were very hard to do because we were affecting families' lives. We justified it by knowing that we saved 97 jobs by cutting 22.

At the end of the first week we found that our problem was $1 million worse than what we already knew to be grim. Our comptroller had $1 million in accounts payable checks printed and in his desk drawer to dole out as cash allowed. The $1 million showed "paid" on the company's balance sheet. I was trying to save a company who had negative net worth! The good news was the company had a $1.8 million loss carry forward. If we could get it profitable we could earn $1.8 million tax free.

Soon the customers knew we were in trouble because they knew of the layoffs and our fill rate (percentage of orders filled) was slipping. I decided honesty was the best policy so despite the protests of others, I made personal visits on the largest customers, told them of our plight and asked for their support while we sorted it out. Thankfully we got the continued support we needed or we would never have made it.

★ BIG LESSON

I've always believed the golden rule is a great business philosophy not just a great religious philosophy. How can you go wrong if you treat customers, suppliers and employees the way you like to be treated?

While fighting through all this we had another problem. Of the roughly 100 total employees, 12 of them in our Portland DC (distribution center) were members of the Teamsters Union. Their contract was up and they wanted more money, more benefits, and to organize the rest of our employees – even though we were close to folding. And if we folded, all the jobs would be gone including the union jobs. The union did not care so they obviously didn't care about their members.

We hired a professional negotiator and he, Bud Coffey (a VP) and I handled the negotiations. It was a long process, but we held our ground in federal mediation (another flawed government process).

Finally we gave them notice that since their contract had expired we were instituting the rules and benefits of our other employees which were collectively better than the union package. We had a great contingency plan put together in case there was a strike and picket lines. Eventually all the union members in our employ resigned from the union and we were free to run our business as our own.

We made the company profitable in the first quarter of 1982, but by then First National Bank of Boston wanted to be rid of us. There were no other banks that would touch us. Fate intervened on our behalf. Ray Sprung had left First National Bank of Boston to head up a new division of First Interstate Bank, First Interstate Commercial Corp – an asset based lending division. We had maintained a friendly relationship with Ray after he left First Boston.

As a new division, they were hungry for new business. We let First Interstate think they took the business away from First Boston. Chris Winters and I structured a leverage buyout of Pacific Wholesalers from the Southworth family and became equal partners. The buyout was financed by First Interstate Commercial Corp. The ownership change was effective Jan. 1, 1983.

Through our national associations we met a brilliant man, Marty Brown, who owned an Automotive Parts Distribution Center in Kansas City. Because cash was tight, we hired him as an outside consultant to help us create cash for our business. He worked with us to devise a plan to get financing from our largest suppliers.

In January of 1984, Chris and I took off on a two-week trip to the east coast to meet with presidents and general managers of some of the world's largest auto parts manufacturers. Companies like Federal Mogul Corp, Standard Motor Products, Sealed Power Corporation, Hasting Manufacturing, Echlin Corp, etc.

> ★ **BIG LESSON**
>
> When you need something that only the top executives can OK – go to them. It buys speed and they "owe you" (law of reciprocity) so they are generally open to your plans.

We were armed with our financial statements, future projections, and a lot of pure resolve. The "what's in it for them" was they would make their largest Northwest distributor healthy in the US's 22nd largest market (Portland). In exchange we would give them loyal support.

Not all of our targeted suppliers agreed to our plan. When they didn't agree, we changed to another brand who would. Our first effort resulted in us gaining $2.1 million in interest free financing for an average term of 34 months. We structured it by accumulating purchases without payment for seven months, and then the total amount was converted to terms of 12, 24, or 36 months depending on the size of the manufacturer and how effectively we negotiated.

An example of a brand change was the changing of our brake parts line from Raybestos to Wagner. At the time our annual purchases from Raybestos were $800,000 a year. When their president told us he could not help us, I really think he was certain we did not have the balls to make a major change.

He was wrong! After that the few others who initially declined to support us financially fell into line. I was described as a "ferocious" negotiator by one CEO. What a great compliment! He did not understand that failure was not an option. I was pretty tough then. I am happy I have mellowed a bit.

I used this strategy again to get another $1 million interest free two years later with the WIFM for the manufacturers being financing new store acquisitions. I also used it in the golf industry where everyone said it could not be done.

As a side note, major brand changes could be very lucrative in those days. The opportunities for supplier financing aren't as prevalent today, but still possible if structured right.

In the next few years our company consolidated into one distribution center in Portland. When we bought the company it was headquartered in Eugene in a 40,000 sq. ft. facility and had a 56,000 sq. ft. branch location Portland. We knew our growth would be in Portland. I moved from Eugene to Portland to let our prospects know how dedicated we were to the Portland market.

Before I left Harr Motor Supply I was going through the chairs of the Oregon Automotive Parts Association. I became president of OAPA about the time we were growing Portland. The press from the industry helped open doors as did the main street press when I had my

Chuck, as president of OAPA, with Oregon Governor Vic Atiyeh

picture taken with Governor Atiyeh or the Mayor of Portland, etc.

> ★ **BIG LESSON**
>
> Dan Kennedy teaches about celebrity value both as the guru and through celebrity association. I did not really get it then, but being OAPA President opened a lot of doors.

I spent most of my time prospecting for new business. Our sales crew could handle picking up a new product line from a store, but I was after ALL their business. Growth was fast.

To accelerate the growth I suggested we have a huge open house and warehouse selling show in Portland. It was billed as "The Best Kept Secret Portland."

A huge amount of planning went into this event. It was choreographed beautifully. Our whole management team consisting of operations manager Karl Southworth, purchasing and data processing manager Dick Harrington, sales manager Don Norberg, marketing manager Don Patterson, Chris, and me were involved.

First we invited the local manufacturer's reps to a meeting at a large suite at the Portland Waterfront Marriott. We served snacks, beer, wine, and booze. Each rep was given a dollar amount they would have to contribute towards the event. They could pay with account credit or free merchandise. We had to strong arm a few, but we got commitments from most so we had our funding.

The warehouse open house and show were at our DC (distribution center) and our social gatherings were at the Marriott. We provided two nights of lodging to out of town customers and invited prospects and one night of accommodations for local customers and invited prospects.

To really set the hook and also establish our show as an annual event I came up with an intriguing offer. We purchased a restored, black, 1957 Ford Thunderbird for $27,500. The car went on our balance sheet as an asset not an expense. This was important because we were still heavily scrutinized by the bank. We announced that we were giving the use of the '57 T-Bird for one year to one lucky attendee.

Then to assure each auto parts store owner went to all the manufactur-ers' booths we gave a $100 bill to each store owner who was verified of stopping at 80 percent of the

The Pacific Wholesaler's 1957 Thunderbird with 2nd year winner, Mike Pease.

booths. To make a show of it we hired an armed security guard to watch the area where the $100 bills were passed out.

The $100 bills were ordered in advance with consecutive serial numbers. At our banquet at the hotel the night of the event we drew the Thunderbird winner by the serial number on the bills. You can imagine the excitement we created because everyone had a chance to win right down to the last couple of numbers.

We also had an oldies band play after the banquet to keep the party atmosphere.

The results were phenomenal. We sold over $400,000 worth of auto parts on that one Saturday the first year. More impor-tantly, we established ourselves as "The Place" to be aligned with.

We brought our crew in and paid them overtime to pull as many of the orders as we could. We even had our delivery trucks deliver the orders on Sunday within 150 miles of Portland. The positive press was fantastic. We truly established our Portland DC as more than a branch.

This event set us up to have an orderly transition from having 40,000 sq. ft. in Eugene, to 10,000 sq. ft., to eventually closing our Eugene facility all together. The inventory investment savings was more than $1 million and the lease and labor savings were huge.

To handle all our business out of Portland we expanded our Portland DC by "going up." We had 56,000 sq. ft. of warehouse space. We double-decked two-thirds of it giving us 93,000 sq. ft. Our landlord built us a free standing office building on adjoining land so we had a true 93,000 sq. ft. of auto parts.

Most of our deliveries were at night. We had keys and alarm codes to over 90 auto parts stores. Our drivers were bonded. Our delivery system was a classic case of operations being a sales asset. I think about this when I hear Dan Kennedy talking about how Disney considers keeping the parks clean a marketing expense.

We requested that stock orders be in our hands by noon, but special orders could be placed by 5 PM and be delivered the

Chuck with Standard Motor Products award at million dollar dinner for purchasing $1 million of Standard products in one year. Note the hair!

same night. It was a fantastic service for our store owners to offer their customers. Imagine that your car broke down in Lakeview, OR and it needed an obscure part. The car dealer might say it would take four days to get the part but our stores would say, "We'll have it when we open at 8 AM tomorrow."

We were operating under the Bumper to Bumper Auto Parts Group at the time. Ten of us who were Bumper to Bumper owners invested $200,000 each to start National Warranty Company. The idea was to allow the installers who were customers of NWC the ability to sell a lifetime warranty on parts and labor to their customers.

This company was not launched on a whim. We conducted focus groups of car owners around the country who said it was a slam dunk. 97.4 percent of our focus group participants said they would purchase our warranty if offered to them. Our projections showed that NWC would be very profitable and that our local distribution center would also grab additional market share.

Two very capable industry executives were hired to build NWC. Indy car driver Rick Mears was hired as spokesman and TV ads were placed in every market that Bumper to Bumper Auto Parts had distribution.

This business was a loser from day one. Not once did we ever hit our monthly projections. In 13 months our $2 million was gone and we were all making monthly contributions to keep it afloat. I was on the board of directors of NWC. I proposed terminating our CEO, buying out the Rick Mears contract, and slashing the national advertising in favor of each Bumper to Bumper distributor advertising locally.

Our "partners" liked the plan and voted in favor of it if I would be the interim CEO. I accepted and commuted from Portland to the NWC office in Nashville once a month. My plan was to shut down NWC fast and minimize further losses. It took six months to get done.

> ★ **BIG LESSON**
>
> To this day I am very skeptical about the results of surveys and particularly focus groups. I've seen more than one focus group or survey give bogus feedback that was costly.

Back at Pacific Wholesalers we were facing tough competition from a co-op distribution company and from discounters. I devised a rebate program for our independents that rewarded them for loyalty to us. It was based on us being the first supplier on major brands in addition to rewarding overall purchase volume. We gained a nice increase in market share. The aforementioned Marty Brown called my plan "brilliant" and asked permission to "steal it" to use in Kansas City.

In the meantime we begin to investigate the possibilities of joining the Carquest Auto Parts cooperative buying and marketing group. The relations with the other Bumper to Bumper owners was deteriorating because of the failure of NWC and we thought Carquest was a stronger group.

This was not a decision to take lightly because we had done a great job of branding Bumper to Bumper throughout Oregon and SW Washington. We would have to replace all the signage at the store level both externally and internally and change over some Bumper to Bumper brands.

Changing to Carquest turned out to be a great decision. Carquest had many more private label brands which were more profitable, had better rebate programs with manufacturers, and had a philosophy of closed distribution in alignment with our own philosophies.

Carquest was run by Dan Bock who was hired by the Carquest DC owners to negotiate with manufacturers for rebates, marketing funds, dedicated representation, and to secure private label programs.

Dan Bock received his input from ownership committees. We all volunteered for or were assigned to committees which met every three months, usually in Chicago, Dallas, or New York. It was there where we forged relationships/friendships with fellow Carquest DC owners.

We owned some very profitable stores of our own and had a great independent jobber base. Our combined sales volume had crossed $25 million per year. If you're keeping score we had doubled the business since we purchased it.

My partnership with Chris was headed south like a bad marriage. I don't know what all the reasons were from his side but from mine it was his ego. Over the years our public personas were that he was the operations guy and I was the sales and marketing guy. This was reinforced because he was a horribly boring public speaker and I was entertaining. I believe he became jealous of some of my achievements.

The reason does not matter because we were 50/50 partners and could not agree on anything. I wanted to continue to grow the business and he wanted the status quo. Our management team was broken up into four directors: sales and marketing, finance, operations, and purchasing. The team and their closest staff members could easily sense that Chris and I were in a different library not just a different page – not a good way to run a nice business.

From the Carquest committees, we became acquainted with Temple Sloan the owner of General Parts in Raleigh, NC. General Parts was the largest Carquest owner by virtue of running a great business and by acquisition. Temple had acquired many Carquest DC's and independents and converted them to Carquest. Temple approached us about buying us because he had no West Coast presence at the time.

We told him our company wasn't for sale but he said we might be surprised at what he would offer. Since Chris and I were in divorce mode, it made sense to listen. After Temple and his staff performed their due diligence, he made an offer that was more than I thought our company was worth. We accepted. The purchase of our company raised the General Parts sales to over $400 million per year. Now, I understand their sales are over $2 billion in the US and Canada.

Chris and I were both offered jobs. Chris immediately accepted and eventually moved to Raleigh, NC. I was offered the position of GM in Milwaukee or the GM of a company about to be purchased in Orlando. While I was considering the pros and cons, Temple told me he appreciated my candor, but in his company I would need to be more of a "yes" man. That made my decision very easy. I said, "I'm gone, I'll take all cash and no stock. I'm moving on." Just the thought of being trapped back in corporate America gave me the chills.

★ BIG LESSON

A note on partnerships or equal stock ownership: Like a marriage, people can tire of each other over time. You have to put up with not just your partner but what's going on in the lives of their spouse and kids, too.

Partners can be a blessing to make funding a deal possible, for complementary talents, and when you're in the "us against the world mode." To avoid the bad times, have frequent discussions about what roles and expectations are.

CHAPTER 8

Incentive Trips

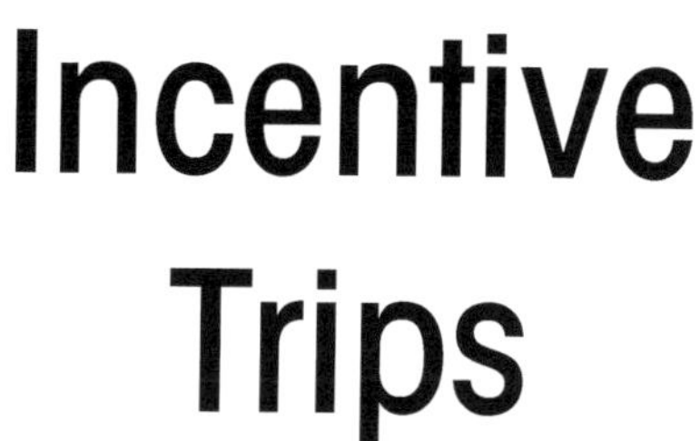

Businesses, regardless of the industry, use incentives to get new business or get an increase in business from their existing customers. I've been on both sides – both receiving incentive trips and devising incentive trips to grow our auto parts business.

The first trips I received were trips to Super Bowl games in Houston and New Orleans when I was working for the Gates Rubber Company. Pacific Wholesalers ran incentive trips for their customers and had a contest for their manufacturer's reps. I won two of them before they discontinued the Super Bowl trips and moved on to other incentive programs.

The second year I won, the game was supposed to be played in the New Orleans Super Dome but it was not finished in time so the game was played in Tulane Stadium. Also the current Dallas –Ft. Worth airport opened on Super Bowl Sunday.

Sixty of us flew to New Orleans on the Friday before the game. The weather was warm and sticky on Friday and Saturday, but on game day it was in the 40s and drizzling, with a nasty wind blowing off the gulf. None of us were dressed for it. I got the idea to buy some Hefty garbage bags to cut the wind and to stay dry. Our seats were scattered throughout the stadium. We put a bag over our feet and another on top with armholes cut in them. The bags kept the four guys I was with dry but not warm.

As a group we had a bloody mary breakfast, drank beer on the bus on the way to the game, and more beer during the game. By the 4th quarter of a very boring football game (The Steelers beat the Vikings) most of the rest rooms in Tulane Stadium were out of order and lines to the few that worked were LONG. Those bags served double duty (if you know what I mean) and the customers sitting with us thought I was a genius!

On the Monday after the game there was a regional meeting in San Francisco for Gates where all the brass was in attendance. Instead of returning to Portland with my group, I flew New Orleans, Dallas, then on to San Francisco on American Airlines. Since it was the first day of the new DFW airport, there were some bugs. The train between terminals stopped and I was trapped with a few others for several hours and missed my flight.

When I got to San Francisco the next morning my suitcase was not with me. So instead of attending the first day of the meetings in a suit and tie, I was in "game day attire," smelly and unshaven. Boy did I have some splainin' to do!

Also on the receiving end of incentive travel, Carol and I had trips to Puerto Vallarta and Ixtapa in Mexico, a trip to Reno, NV on Fram's private plane, two trips to Caesar's Palace in Las Vegas, a trip to Montreal, two trips to Pebble Beach, and a few others I don't even remember.

On the Montreal trip Chris and his wife and Carol and I were with owners of several other auto parts distribution companies. One of the speakers was Senator Thomas Eagleton of Missouri. Sen. Eagleton was George McGovern's running mate for a few weeks in his presidential campaign.

Our group was taken on a side trip by bus to Quebec City. Sen. Eagleton was on my bus and he and I hit it off. We did not talk politics because he and I were on opposite sides of the "aisle." On the way back to Montreal we were pretty bored so I encouraged the bus driver to stop at a convenience store to buy some beer. My stuffy partner, Chris and his wife were dying of embarrassment and said something to me. Sen. Eagleton told them I had a great idea and that he wanted a beer also. So the senator and I got off the bus together, walked into a convenience store where the French-Canadian clerks pretended they did not speak any English and bought a couple of cases of beer for our bus mates. What a gas!

> ★ **BIG LESSON**
>
> You can find common ground with most people if you take the time to get to know them.

On our Pebble Beach trips I served on a Wagner Distributor advisory council. Since they were getting free advice from their customers who were freely giving up their time, the "perks" were great. We stayed at the Lodge at Pebble Beach and signed all our expenses to our room. I flew in a day early and played golf at the Pebble Beach Golf Links and at Spy Glass Hills Golf Links. We'd have ½ day meetings and then play golf at Pebble Beach in the afternoon and then have a great dinner at the lodge. They also took care of the ladies. They went on local excursions and played golf, too. Carol made par on the famous 7th hole on her first round at Pebble Beach.

I love the Pebble Beach golf course because of all the history surrounding it and because I've played it at least 14 times. My favorite hole in golf is #8 at Pebble. In fact, when I pass I've asked my ashes be scattered off the cliff in the middle of the dog leg to the beach below.

We also devised incentive earn back trips for customers and prospects. In the auto parts days I planned and hosted trips to the Silverado Resort in Napa, CA, La Costa Resort in Carlsbad, CA, Reno, NV, multiple trips to Hawaii, two Caribbean cruises, and many other fun trips. These were all designed to pay for the trip with a combination of manufacturer's money and a small part of the additional gross profit we made on the sales increase.

I have a few stories I want to share here because they teach the necessity of being tough when you have to be and also teach the need for creativity.

When we changed from Raybestos brakes to Wagner brake products we negotiated a war chest of incentives to be paid for by Wagner to make sure our auto parts store customers made the change with us.

We had a tough old SOB (said with true affection), Toby Taucher, who owned a large store in Albany, OR. He was holding out because he did not want the hassle of a change and was not moved by the incentives. He was an avid golfer but I did not know him very well at the time and had never played golf with him.

The retired GM of our Portland DC, Neil Imes, had been close to Toby over the years. I persuaded Wagner to send their regional sales manager, Neil, Toby, and I to Pebble Beach Golf Links for four rounds of golf at Pebble, Spyglass, and two other Monterey Peninsula courses. Then I had to convince Neil and Toby to go. Neil said he wasn't good enough to play those courses and Toby said I couldn't bribe him with golf. I finally convinced them both to go and assured Toby he was not committing to change to Wagner.

Of course we had a great time and I built a solid relationship with Toby that lasted for years. About four months after our golf trip he made the change. We sent Toby and his wife on a Caribbean cruise as their incentive.

Another hard to get guy on the Wagner changeover was Doug Updenkelder. Doug, whom had become a good personal friend, owned stores in Newport and Lincoln City, OR. Friend or not he was a tough sale. I knew he would not care about our TV, Hawaii, or cruise incentives so I got creative. Knowing he was an avid hunter and fisherman helped.

The value of the incentive Doug would qualify for was $5,000. We met in the restaurant at Agate Beach Golf Course and I went through my pitch. I pulled each incentive sheet out of my folder, showed it to him and said, "But I know you don't want this" and threw the sheet over my shoulder onto the floor.

Then I said, "I have a special incentive for you." I put a new attaché case in front of him. I opened it to reveal $5,000 in $100 dollar bills and a .32 caliber pistol on top of the money. I said, "this is your changeover incentive." He checked to see if the pistol was loaded and eyed the money like it might not be real.

> ### ★ BIG LESSON
>
> In business being unpredictable can be used to great advantage. Your employees, customers and suppliers always have to pay attention to you.

Our last big incentive trip for our customers was to the island of Moorea in Tahiti. We had some "heartburn" along the way caused by my not taking enough time to check out the travel agency.

Our customers loved the Tahiti destination so creating an earn back program that was profitable for us was not a problem. When you create an earn back offer, you always want to have a long earn back period to allow smaller accounts a chance to participate and to have long term excitement. In this case the earn back period was 10 months.

We sent post cards, pictures of paradise, cashews (they grow them in Tahiti), coconuts, etc. to our customers and prospects on a regular basis to keep interest high. We'd paid the travel agency a small deposit up front and then a $10,000 deposit about six months before the trip for the French airline, UTA. Three months before the trip I called the travel agency. Shock! No answer!

I found the owners at home. The wife was in "seclusion" and her husband told me their business had failed and our $10,000 had NOT been paid to the airline. I was not accepting the fact that we were going to lose $10,000 and went into intimidation mode. Rarely is that a good strategy but in this case it worked.

Two days later he called me to set up a meeting with me and a travel industry buddy of his, Roger McBride, who owned a good-sized travel agency. Roger agreed to step in and pay the airline if we would agree to use his agency for all our travel for two years.

In the long run everything worked out.

★ 2 BIG LESSONS

#1 Know whom you're dealing with. For a $60,000 trip, I should have done more due diligence on the travel agent.

#2 Always be tenacious. If I had just accepted their explanation, we'd have lost $10,000.

CHAPTER 9

The Golf Biz Years

So now I again had the opportunity to decide what I wanted to be when I grew up. I left Carquest Portland in June of 1992. My daughter, Amy, was on the junior golf circuit in Oregon. One of the enjoyable things I had a chance to do was travel Oregon and Washington with Carol and Amy to junior golf tournaments. I would never have had the time if we had not sold the company.

While traveling I was giving a lot of thought to the next phase of my life. I had head hunters calling me about "turn arounds" in the auto parts world. I seriously considered the GM job at an American Parts DC in Fairfield, CA. Their sales were horrid. I knew I could ramp them up fast with my style of leadership and make a huge bonus. However, my disdain for working in corporate America protected me from accepting the position.

I looked at some small manufacturing companies in Oregon. One of them manufactured fuel caps for large trucks and off road equipment. Ironically, one of their customers was the Gates Rubber Company. The negotiations ended when

I became suspicious of the information the CFO was feeding me. It turned out he wanted to purchase the company and saw me as a rival.

My loves at the time were boating and golf. I always thought the golf equipment retailers in Portland were an arrogant bunch with no customer service skills. I considered purchasing a marina on Puget Sound in Washington, but eventually decided on opening golf stores in Portland.

I decided to purchase an International Golf, Inc franchise. I chose a franchise because my research showed that getting an open account with the biggest companies in golf – Titleist, Callaway, TaylorMade, Ping, etc. would be damn near impossible as an independent.

There were Nevada Bob's and Pro Golf Franchises in Portland so they were not options. Besides, in gathering information about franchises, I posed as a prospective franchisee whom was willing to move to another city to open stores. The Pro Golf franchise manager lied to me on several key points.

> ★ **BIG LESSON**
>
> Mystery shop everything! Your business, your competitors, and EVEN prospective suppliers or business partners.

With the help of Steve Porter, the CEO of International Golf Enterprises, we found a great location in a crappy building on 82nd Ave in Portland close to a regional shopping mall, Clackamas Town Center.

The location was great but the free standing building was a piece of junk. I had to show my remodel and tenant improvement plans to the Clackamas County Commission for Clackamas Town Center to get approval to have a business in the special shopping center zone. I was well prepared and that's a good tip – like the Boy Scouts, "Always be prepared."

I came to the meeting with my plans and artist renderings but ALSO pictures of the eye sore of a building on 82nd Ave. The exterior of the building was painted light brown and had been painted with rollers and paint brushes. The building had been vacant so grass was growing up in the gravel parking lot. It looked like hell.

Typical of under achieving bureaucrats, the commission put me through the ringer. I had already signed the lease with the owner, but I finally showed the commission the pictures of the building and then my renderings showing a freshly painted white building with green trim, a paved parking lot, and a small grassy area between the two driveways. I said, "I haven't signed the lease yet. If you don't approve my plan you'll continue to have an eye sore across the street from your shopping center. I have not signed the lease, so it's your call."

They voted in favor with one dissenter. The dissenter was the environmental guy on the commission who thought I should be forced to spend $30,000 in landscaping for a 4,000 sq. ft. building.

★ BIG LESSON

The more prepared you are the better negotiator you are.

The next hurdle was the building inspectors. There was a four-week backlog to approve building permits. I found out the fine for not having a permit was the doubling of the permit fee. The original permit was $350 so I figured paying an extra $350 to save four weeks was a bargain. My concern was pissing the inspector off and not getting my Certificate of Occupancy in a timely fashion.

When the inspector finally showed up we were 90 percent done with the improvements. The contractor was installing slot wall at the time. I played very dumb and very humble. I told him since I was only installing fixtures (slot wall) I did not think I needed a permit. In fact we had done a whole lot more. I paid the double permit fee, made a couple of minor changes the inspector wanted and received the COO.

There happened to be a Nevada Bob's store two blocks from the location. At the time I was a member at Pleasant Valley Country Club. The owner of the Nevada Bob's store told my friends at the club he would put me out of business by cutting his prices 20 percent. How is that for a ridiculous strategy? He does not know me, my finances or my business experience but he is going to cut prices in his store selling $200,000 a month. Or – it cost him $40,000 a month and me nothing because I have just opened and have no sales.

Managing golf stores is a serious business. The inventory investment is huge, you must have purchasing and inventory control experience, you have a lot of employees to baby sit, you have to have great marketing and advertising skills, and you have to have the ability to "work" your suppliers. My 16 years of auto parts experience were a tremendous asset.

We opened the first golf store in Nov. of 1992. I had quite a tax obligation because of the sale of Carquest, so any loss I showed in the golf store would be going against my personal tax liability. I spent far and away more money in advertising the last six weeks of the year than would normally be prudent. Because of the overall tax savings it was like getting a 50 percent discount on whatever I spent on promotion.

The night before the store opened I held a private party for all of my friends and acquaintances. They were invited with a fancy golf theme invitation mailed to their homes and offices. We served over 200 people that night and got great word-of-mouth for our "soft" grand opening.

In March of 1993, we had our official grand opening. It was like the cliché from the movie, *Field of Dreams,* "Build it and they will come." I visualized the parking lot full, the store crammed with people and the cash register buzzing. That is exactly what happened. People were parking two and three blocks away and walking to the store.

The Nevada Bob's owner had spent over $100,000 to "put me out of business" and we were kicking his rear. That was fun! In four short months we went from being a "who?" to a force on the east side of Portland. The price cutting from Nevada Bob's stopped and we peacefully co-existed.

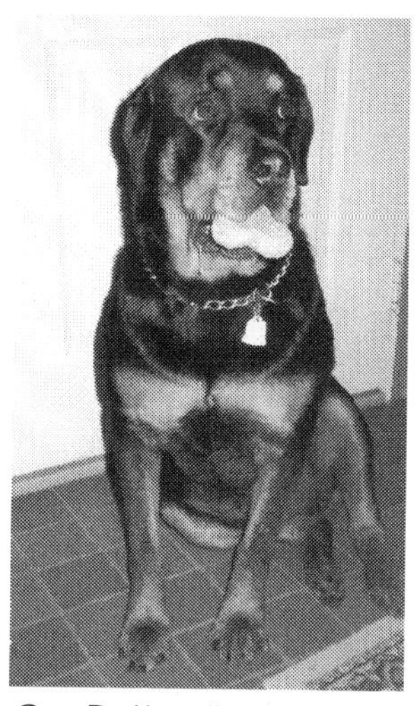
Our Rottweiler "Minnie" in 1993.

For those who have been to Portland, you know the east wind can really blow on the east side in winter. Sometimes it rattled the doors so hard it set off our security alarm. In the early days, before I had store managers, I was #1 on the call list for the alarm company. We had a 105-pound Rottweiler named Minnie. She was a pussycat, but a 105-pound Rottweiler is still imposing. When I answered alarm calls in the middle of the night, Minnie and I generally arrived before the police. I'd send Minnie in first. We were broken into a few times but Minnie and I never did get to catch anybody.

Knowing that to effectively market golf equipment in Portland, I would have to have a west side presence. In February of 1993, again with the help of Steve Porter, I found a 5,000 sq. ft. location in a small strip mall in Beaverton. We opened the Beaverton location in April of 1993 and followed that up with a location in Hillsboro a couple of years later.

Speaking of dogs and break-ins, once in our Beaverton store the cops were nearby when the alarm sounded. The robber ran and was taken down by a police dog outside the main door. I asked my crew to leave the blood on the ground for a couple of days with a little sign telling what happened as a deterrent against future theft. Once a Marine always a Marine!

Over the next few years we built our golf business through multi-media marketing and through sound, and enforced, customer relations strategies. The key was ENFORCED! You have to teach your employees how you want things done and then be sure they do it your way. I am a firm believer in the use of mystery shoppers for all businesses not just retail businesses.

> ## ★ BIG LESSON
>
> There is an old cliché, "inspect what you expect." It is so true with employees. You have to spell out exactly how things are to be done and then catch them doing things right to reinforce the behavior. That and use mystery shoppers.

The second time any employee told a customer "according to company policy" they were FIRED! I believe the golden rule business philosophy empowers employees to make the right customer service decisions. If you honestly treat someone exactly how you would like to be treated, how can you go wrong? If employees gave away too much to solve a customer issue they would be trained on how to handle future issues, but never reprimanded.

I sincerely believe the #1 reason we became the market leader so quickly was the empowerment of employees to make smart customer service decisions.

Back to multi-media marketing. We used newspaper, radio, television, billboards, newsletters, interviews, sponsorships, golf trade shows, shopping services, and much more. We made our TV commercials in our stores and featured our employees. I never featured myself because our customers had a much better chance of being helped by my staff than me.

I ran TV commercials on local segments of national golf telecasts. I also always bid for last minute unsold time for the major events like the Masters and US Open. I always got at least 1 spot with this strategy. The stations would offer the spots in advance for $3,500 for a 30-second spot. I would bid $300. I got last minute calls from the TV stations every time either accepting the $300 or countering with $400 or $500. It's a good strategy.

We also received co-op advertising money from TaylorMade once for putting a TaylorMade driver on the sides of several articulated city buses with our store locations mentioned prominently. Another effective, but obscure campaign was Water Closet Media. We had International Golf ads displayed above the urinals in high traffic sports bars.

Another interesting retail strategy was personal shopping services. We had several customers who were business owners or CEO's of large companies. I developed a relationship with them and then kept their credit card info in a private file. For Christmas, birthdays, client gifts, etc., they would call me with the names and addresses and golf gifts they wanted shipped. We literally sold hundreds-of-thousands of dollars of golf equipment and shipped it all over the country.

We tried two other strategies to grow the business. The first was putting one of our stores inside a driving range. The owner of the range was Chuck Milne. Chuck was a very good local pro who later played on the European Senior Tour. We sold a lot of golf equipment but also experienced a lot more theft than we did in our purely retail stores.

Milne was well known and liked by everyone. He introduced me to a lot of local golf pros including Pat Fitzsimons. Pat was a great player on the regular PGA tour in the 70s and won the LA Open in 1974.

My friendships with Chuck and Fitz got me playing in local Pro-Ams and opened some other doors for me. They introduced me to Larry Giusti who sponsored a "major" for local pros every April with some serious prize money for a local event.

We became a sponsor of the International Golf Pro-Am at the Giusti Memorial. Our sponsorship was appreciated by the local pros and it led to us being the only retail golf equipment store ever endorsed by the Northwest PGA. Usually discount stores and golf course pro shops have an adversarial relationship.

> ★ **BIG LESSON**
>
> Work hard on developing relationships with those you like - doors can open for you. Chuck, Fitz and I all benefited from the friendship we developed.

In 1998 the absentee owner of the Pro Golf Store on the Portland west side died. I was proactive in contacting his wife and her advisors. They sold me the assets and assigned me the lease. The location and store size were better than my Beaverton location and my Beaverton lease had six months left. We operated both stores in Beaverton for the six months and then moved the Beaverton inventory.

We had quite a campaign to bring over the Beaverton customers. We were very successful with it. There was some pain in getting the inherited staff to do things the International Golf way, but after a couple of casualties (terminations) and a lot of team building on the golf course, we got everyone in sync.

Because the merger created so much extra inventory we had a tent sale to get the cash out of the goods. It was so successful it became an annual event. In our best year we sold over $400,000 in three days at the one location. We served hot dogs, soft drinks, and had clowns and the Portland Trail Blazer mascot for the kids. We also had a few of the Blazer dancers for the adult male children and awesome door prizes! We had a huge advertising blitz, too. As you probably suspect by now this was all paid for with free goods from the manufacturers.

Later we put one of our stores inside the pro shop of Columbia Edgewater Country Club. It was prestigious for us and a home run for the Columbia Edgewater membership and the club itself. The deal was that I would not pay rent, but I would pay the club 10 percent of sales and have one of my staff members in their shop at busy times.

I bought their inventory so they had no inventory investment. CE members could buy at the club and charge it to their club account or buy from our retail stores and use their club account. Either way the club received credit for the sale.

The arrangement worked great until there was a changing of the guard at the club. The GM, head pro Dan Hixon, and the club president of their board of directors, all changed within a few months of each other. The incoming club president was John Zupan. Zupan owned a chain of supermarkets in the Portland area and had an ego the size of Texas and enjoyed his position of power at Columbia Edgewater.

My contract with CE ended at the end of October. Zupan convinced me to keep my store at the club until March while he "sorted things out." I had a gut feeling we were going to get screwed, but I agreed to stay. Sure enough the contract was not renewed even though financially, it was a better deal for the club. John Zuppan could not stand to have my team running the CE pro shop. The four extra months we kept the shop were the worst months of the year for golf equipment sales so we lost our butts.

★ **BIG LESSON**

Your gut is right most of the time – trust it.

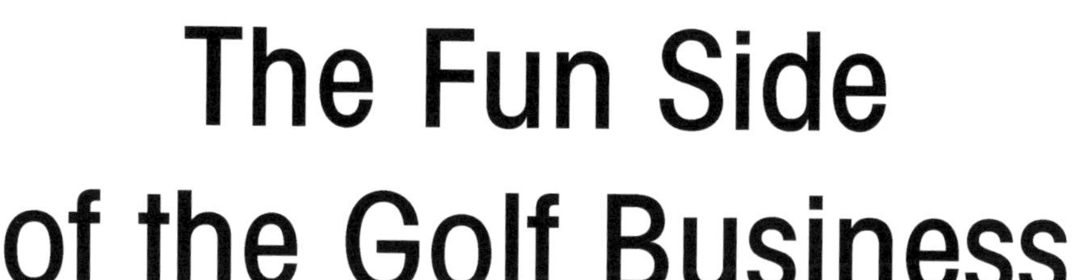

CHAPTER 10

The Fun Side of the Golf Business

Like the auto parts business, the golf business was very good to me. At different times I was a guest of Titleist in both their MA locations and ball and club fitting facilities in CA. I have received putting tips from Scotty Cameron and wedge play tips from Bob Vokey. I have been a guest of Callaway many times. Lynx invited me to an outing at the PGA show in Orlando where I played three holes with Fred Couples.

I played in four LPGA pro-ams as a guest of Ping and Nike. All the pros I played with, worked hard to make it fun for the amateurs. Cathy Johnson-Forbes made an ace on the 16th hole after we ams all missed the green badly. We could tell from the scoreboard we were in the hunt and all choked. We said, "C'mon Cathy, knock it stiff." One bounce, hit the stick and in the hole – really exciting to see.

Kelli Kuehne was another LPGA player who showed us a great time. She was about 5'2" and weighed about 120 lbs. Everyone in our group tried to out drive her but never did. I thought I got her on number 10. When I teased her about finally out driving her, she showed me her club. She'd teed off with a 3-wood! Kelli also has Type 1 diabetes. She wore the pump during the pro-am. It was interesting to hear her talk about how she regulated it for her adrenaline levels in competition.

I also played in Peter Jacobsen's Fred Meyer Challenge as a guest of Nike. Our pro was Tommy Armour III and our celebrity player was Green Bay Packer football star, Sterling Sharpe. Both told incredible stories. It's really weird to have hundreds of people lining a fairway to see the celebs and trusting you not to slice or hook a ball into them. They don't know how bad it hurts to get smacked in the head with a golf ball.

Speaking of Peter Jacobsen, I have a cool story about the 1995 Ryder Cup played at Oak Hill in Rochester, NY. Peter made the team that year. He designed Oregon Golf Club where three of my friends, Bill Johnston, Robert Jack, and Mike Concannon were members. I was an acquaintance of Peter's from University of Oregon fund raisers.

About 10 days before the Ryder Cup began, the four of us decided to attend. We called Peter's office at PJP productions and Peter gave us free passes to the Ryder Cup and a "To Whom It May Concern" letter that named us each by name and ask that as friends and members of his club we be extended the same professional courtesies the reader would extend to him.

We could not get a room in Rochester. The nearest place we found any decent hotels was in Lockport, NY about 60 miles away. That turned out to be a huge break as you'll soon see.

We flew a red eye from Portland to Chicago to Buffalo. The new TaylorMade Burner Bubble drivers arrived in our golf stores the day before. Rain was pouring in Buffalo, but we decided to try to use our Peter Jacobsen letter at the Country Club of Buffalo. The letter worked great and the head pro comped golf and carts for the four of us. Instead of warming

One of the food tents at the 1995 Ryder Cup in Rochester, NY.

up we went right to the first tee. The brand new, never been hit driver, slipped out of my hands went under the ball and left a huge "scar" in the paint on the top plate. The driver flew 30 yards, the ball went 10 yards, and my buddies were rolling in laughter on the wet grass.

That afternoon we drove to Lockport and showed the head pro at the Lockport Country Club our PJ letter. He gave us an early comped tee time for the next morning. When we arrived the GM and the club president of Lockport CC met us at the golf shop. They told us we would have membership privileges for the four days we would be there. Sweet!

The next four days we would either play in the morning and watch the Ryder cup in the afternoon or go to the Ryder Cup early and play back at Lockport late in the afternoon.

There were sponsors' hospitality tents everywhere. I had 1 pass to the PGA tent which was given to me by Miller Golf Bags. Johnnie Walker also had a tent. Their guests were all given a black jacket with "Johnnie Walker" logos embroidered on them in yellow. Robert offered one of the guests $100 for his jacket and ended up buying it for $200.

Johnny Walker did not check the credentials of anyone wearing one of their jackets so Robert had access to their tent. We quickly found that my PGA credential from Miller Bag would get me in any of the hospitality tents. We enjoyed a lot of great liquor and food with our run of the grounds.

Robert was in the trucking business. We found that Cummins Engine Company also had a hospitality tent. While in their tent we met Gary McClain who owns Interstate Trucking out of Washington state. It turned out that Gary had picked up the Cummins executives in his Gulfstream and flew them out to Rochester.

From that meeting, Gary McClain became a customer for my "private client" services at International Golf. Occasionally we played a round of golf. Once I played with Gary and Robert at Sun River in Central Oregon. Gary decided he wanted an In-N-Out Burger so he had his pilots fly Robert and him to Scottsdale. I had to return to Portland that night so I missed out on the $5,000 hamburger.

★ BIG LESSON

Opportunity always knocks when you are open to it. I was on a lark enjoying the Ryder Cup experience, but because I was with other business people we discussed a lot of business. Then bang! I'm sipping scotch with a new corporate client. Keep "open" at all times.

My favorite golf equipment manufacturer was TaylorMade. Our local rep, Fred Barr was a great rep and the top management team was smart, aggressive and fun to be around. The chairman was a young Adidas Exec, Jim Stutts, and the CEO was and still is Mark King. Mark is a real visionary, an aggressive deal maker and a man with great instincts. Under his leadership, TaylorMade has grown from $300 million to $1.2 billion in annual sales.

Twice, I was invited to play in the TaylorMade pro-am in Cabo San Lucas. The first time I was in a group with Mike Wan. Mike was the VP of Sales for TaylorMade in those days. Now Mike is the commissioner of the LPGA. Our pro was Steve Porter whom I mentioned earlier and our 4th player was Jack Lane, who unfortunately is no longer with us. Aldila, a golf club shaft manufacturer, was paying $1,000 for every skin on the first day of the tourney. Jack Lane and I agreed that if either of us earned a skin (highly unlikely we thought) we would split the cash. I knocked in a 7-iron from 155 yards on a par 4 for eagle and made a birdie for a net eagle on a par 5 that somehow held up for a 2nd skin. Jack was happy as hell we made that agreement.

In 2000 my company won a TaylorMade contest. The prize was an all-expense paid trip for two to the 2000 US Open at Pebble Beach. I invited my friend, Bill Johnston, as my guest. My family had a trip planned to Scotland and Bill's family had reservations in Paris in early June.

Carol and I were in Edinburg with our daughter, Tara, her husband Alex, and our brand new granddaughter, Gretta.

Bill flew over from Paris to Edinburgh a few days before we were due at the US Open. We played golf with a friend of mine, Gordon Bell, who lived in Edinburgh and also happened to be the master blender for Johnnie Walker.

On the Sunday before the US Open, I played St Andrews with Alex's cousin who was a member. It was a very benign day (2-club wind) and I took a few quid off the Scots. On Tuesday, Bill and I played St Andrews in gale force winds. We couldn't even get a caddy because they did not want to go out in the wind. It was incredibly hard.

On the Wednesday before the US Open we flew to San Francisco. TaylorMade put us up in the downtown Hyatt

Regency. My local rep, Fred Barr, entertained us on Wednesday night. We were too jet lagged to be much fun. It was the week of record heat in San Francisco. It was 102 degrees instead of the normal 55 that night. We ate in an authentic Chinese restaurant in China Town with no air conditioning.

The next day Fred drove us down to Pebble Beach. TaylorMade provided lodging for several of their guests in the Carmel Valley Lodge. They bussed us to either the golf tournament or to local golf courses where they had pre-arranged tee times. They also had a hospitality tent at Pebble Beach.

Bill and I played golf in the mornings and went to the golf tournament in the afternoons. Our strategy, one I still use to watch PGA Tour events, was to watch the leaders on the front nine, catch some of the other players on the back nine, and then retreat to the hospitality tent to watch the leaders finish their rounds on TV. The tournament had no drama – it was the year that Tiger won by 12 strokes.

The day after the tournament, TaylorMade had tee times for us at Pebble Beach in US Open conditions. The rough was so deep that we couldn't advance the ball when we hit it in there. It gave us a real appreciation for how strong the pros are.

Our caddy was a young guy who said he was Clint Eastwood's regular caddy at Pebble. He told some great stories and kept us entertained during a very long round with lots of waiting between shots.

My claim to fame is that on my golf resume I played the most storied golf courses in the world, St. Andrews and Pebble Beach in the same week.

CHAPTER 11

Winding Down International Golf

From 1992 through 2000, we built our company from a start up with 0 sales to a market leader with over $10 million in annual sales. It was hard work with lots of failures along with great successes. I met and worked with some wonderful people.

The 9-11 terrorist attacks had a very negative effect on the golf industry. People's mindset was to hold onto their money and, understandably, spend time with their families. The business went from hard work but fun to just hard work and one challenge after another.

In 2003 I decided to sell. It took a year to find a buyer. Unfortunately the buyer thought he "knew it all" and went out of business quickly. I offered to consult with him for a year for free. He did not want any advice. He immediately dumped the franchise, changed the name of the company, and replaced some key employees with "his people."

> ### ★ BIG LESSON
>
> Another cliché: "Don't knock down the fences before you know why they were built." Why would the new owner change the name and the key people of a successful business on day one?

In the long run I don't fault him for any of these decisions. I do fault him for making these changes in the first 60 days after he purchased the business. You just don't drop a respected name in a market because you did not choose it. Name changes must be thought out and strategized so as not to confuse the regular customer base.

CHAPTER 12

Internet Marketing– The Early Days

In those days there were lots of rules governing selling big name golf equipment on the internet. Web sites were pretty new and email marketing was in its infancy, too. There was pay per click advertising it just wasn't Google. You could easily tell what everyone was bidding per click.

Our International Golf site was just a brochure. We were not allowed to put product with prices on the site. To get around the factory rules we built a couple of rogue sites.

Tour Edge is a relatively unknown small manufacturer who makes high quality equipment. They had a driver named "Bazooka." We found that Tour Edge was paying 5¢ a click for "Tour Edge" and "Bazooka." They directed prospects to local retailers across the US by zip code.

We purchased the URL Bazooka.com and bid 6¢ a click to get to the #1 spot. We used the exact product description from the Tour Edge catalog and put a small sales blurb on the site and shipped Bazookas all over the country.

One day a web customer from Chicago (Tour Edge is in Chicago) insisted on talking to the owner. He wanted to mail me a cashier's check for a Bazooka and have me ship it to his office when the check arrived. I gave him all the BS about how secure our credit card processing was on the web site, etc. He said, "You don't get it. My wife sees my credit card statements, but she never would notice a new driver in my golf bag." I shipped his driver out BEFORE I got the check. That kind of golfer is honest!

> ★ **BIG LESSON**
>
> Most of the time it's best to shut up and listen rather than try to display your knowledge. The man had a simple problem that I tried to overcomplicate. I told this story in web page copy and we received several orders by phone with cashier's checks mailed to us.

We started another rogue site called BirdieBoys.com to sell name brand equipment at a discount. We ran small display ads in Golf Digest magazine for $5,000 a month. For every dollar we spent in advertising we got a dollar in sales. With cost of goods running 70 percent we were losing $1,500 a month on our Golf Digest ad.

After five months I pulled the plug on the ad. The next month Golf Digest had an article on the best golf equipment sites on the internet. They rated BirdieBoys.com in the top five sites. We sold almost $50,000 that month and had a couple of good months after that.

Since then I've sold many products and services on the internet amounting to a ton of money. It's still a thrill to see the emails come in that say, "On Line Shopping Cart Order." It's just as much fun as getting a check in the mail.

Retirement? No way in Hell!

After the post 9-11 years I thought I was ready for an early retirement. Man, was I wrong! I found the only guys playing golf on weekday mornings were guys 20 years older than me who had lost their zest for life. I could not stand not being "in the business game" every day.

CHAPTER 13

Failure!

I met Ron Cardwell in Austin. Ron was successful in the low end of the real estate business. He bought repossessed manufactured homes from mortgage companies, rehabbed them, and set them up on one to five acre home sites. He sold them for an absurd profit (said with affection). He often netted 70 percent profit on a deal.

His plan appealed to me and so did the return on investment. I set out to emulate his success. A friend in Idaho sent me information about a housing shortage in my target market's price range in the Lewiston – Clarkston area. At the time remodeled manufactured homes on a nice lot were selling for $110,000.

Long story short, I bought a nice ½ acre lot in Clarkston, WA and bought a repossessed 24 X 60 ft. manufactured home in Beaverton, Oregon. I was my own "contractor" on the job.

I decided to put in a real foundation, not the typical cement blocks spaced out under the home. Because I had a great lot on a hill overlooking a golf course and because I poured a "real" foundation, my local real estate guy and I thought the place would sell for $125,000. I expected to have $62,000 invested in the deal.

The two halves of the unit were towed to my lot and placed on my foundation. I was there when it was delivered. The neighbors who all lived in "stick built" houses went ballistic when they saw the manufactured home delivered in their sub division. I obviously had the permits to do the project, but the neighborhood was still mad as hell.

Simultaneously, I bought a beautiful five acre piece of land in Smithville, TX. It is gorgeous country property with a mixture of oak and pine trees on it. Then I bought another repossessed 24 x 65 ft. manufactured home. I expected to have $45,000 invested in this deal. Comparable sales in the area were $105,000 to $115,000.

The cost overruns were killing me as the real estate market started a rapid decent and financing for my potential buyers was drying up.

I eventually sold the Clarkston property in 2008. After holding for 18 months, I lost money on it and that's not even factoring in the value of my time. I still have the Texas property as a rental.

> ## ★ BIG LESSON
>
> Don't start a business you know nothing about. Work for or partner with somebody with experience to get an education in the industry.

The Texas deal has a side story. One day I received a telephone call from my real estate listing agent. She took a prospective buyer to the home to show it. She said the home had been freshly vandalized and she was afraid and leaving quick.

We lived 45 minutes away. After calling the sheriff, I loaded a small arsenal of weapons (a 12 gauge shotgun and two pistols – a .32 automatic and a.357 revolver) into the car and headed to the property.

When we got there I was sick. The vandals had thrown fresh paint on the walls and carpet, ripped holes in the sheet rock walls, poured paint on the stove and refrigerator, and smashed plumbing fixtures with a hammer. I was furious. It is lucky they were not around because if they had given me any BS I probably would have used my weapons.

When the sheriff drove up, I hid my weapons under a blanket in the car. After he wrote down my information, he informed me that in Texas, I would be within my legal rights to shoot the vandals on my property even if they were running away. You gotta love Texas!

Government Contractor?

While I was trying to be a real estate investor, I also failed in a government contracting business. I spent $10,000 to get the business model, contact lists, and two days of training.

I set up an LLC where the owners were my wife, two daughters and me. I had all the basics covered – women/ veteran owned company.

The business consists of becoming an approved government contractor, and then bidding on everything they may need to buy. I specialized in bidding on items put out to bid by military bases. I would research where I could buy items put out to bid and then quote them.

On the first order I received, I discovered that they required specialized packaging and inspection of the goods and packaging. I spent more on packaging than I made on the deal.

After that I bid everything as standard commercial packaging. We were disqualified from a lot of deals, but I didn't have to allow for unknown packaging costs when I bid. I understand the need for special packaging and inspection of electronic parts that might be going on a ship, but not for everyday items. That's why we hear reports of $25 rolls of toilet paper.

This business was too time consuming and required too much rear end kissing of government purchasing agents for me.

Success Again

As luck would have it (I believe we make our own luck) I was approached by an auto parts store owner and golf retailer at about the same time. They heard I was retired and offered to pay my expenses to look over a couple of little problems they wanted fixed. I was flattered and jumped at the chance to help them. When a few more requests came in from other business owners to do more consulting, I started charging for my services. That's the simple story of how I became a consultant.

The auto parts store owner was not pleased to learn that his cash flow problems were created by airline tickets and nights at the Fairmont Hotel in San Francisco. I chastised him for living an extravagant personal life out of his store's checkbook. While he was launching a new machine shop, his wife was entertaining a lover in style. Sometimes a consultant has to deliver bad news!

It turns out that I have a knack for consulting. My 35 years of diverse business experience allows me to see opportunities within a business that the owners don't consider in their own businesses.

The only way for America to become great again is for small business to prosper. I believe it is my current life's purpose to use my experience and talent to help businesses to succeed.

> **Opportunity:** If you need fresh "outside eyes" to look over your business, call my office at 480-773-7490 and schedule a phone conference to see if we're a fit to work together.

CHAPTER 15

The Dan Kennedy Years

My first recollection of studying Dan Kennedy style direct response marketing was in 2000. I purchased Dan's *Magnetic Marketing* home study course. I don't remember how I learned about it, maybe from someone who attended a success seminar where Dan spoke for nine years. Even today, the updated version is a must for anyone wanting to begin to learn direct response marketing. Check out http:// JumboMarketingTools.com/ for your copy.

Something about the course resonated with me. It was like Dan was talking to me one on one. It was reassuring to know I was already employing many of his strategies, but of greater value were strategies that were new to me – simple things like multiple touches, segmenting lists, etc.

In the auto parts stores our wholesale customer list was our accounts receivable list. I also tracked wholesale cash customers through my accounts receivable. I regularly sent newsletters and specials to these customers, but I did not build a list or communicate with my retail customers. Dan

Dan Kennedy and Chuck in Phoenix in 2009.

Kennedy's teachings made me realize how much money I left on the proverbial table – hundreds of thousands of dollars in sales I'm sure.

Even before I started studying Dan's materials, I kept a half assed list of my retail golf customers. After Dan, I went on a mission to build a good list – niched where possible. I paid a spiff (commission) of 25¢ to my retail sales staff for every name they added to our list. Some of my folks were making an extra $50 a month by collecting names. I never penalized them for duplicates from multiple stores because I did not want to discourage their good behavior.

We sent a monthly newsletter and specials to this list. We emailed them a copy of our weekly newspaper ads a day before they were in the paper, and coupons and invitations to private events to these captured email addresses.

As a side note, I recently used this strategy with one of my private clients, Wave Fashion. I convinced Jae Shin to pay his stores' retail staff 50¢ a name. Wave added 1,500 names in the first 90 days and the list keeps growing. You can make a lot of "cashola" from 1,500 new names.

Another way I used our list was for private sales. Our private sales were real private sales. We actually closed our stores early, covered the windows and doors with brown paper and brought in food and drinks. We encouraged our customers to bring their golfing friends and spend the evening with us. We had putting contests on our indoor putting green and drawings for prizes. We packed 'em in, showed 'em a good time, and of course sold a boat load of merchandise.

All the first timers in the store were added to our list and they invited their friends to subsequent private sales.

> ★ **BIG LESSON**
>
> Some businesses try to run a private sale or a customer appreciation sale during regular business hours or have it open to the public. DON'T DO IT! Make it special for your customers and they will be loyal to you forever.

In the spring of 2008 we were living in Cedar Park, TX a suburb of Austin. A new Glazer-Kennedy IBA (Independent Business Advisor) invited those on the Austin GKIC list to her first meeting. I attended and enjoyed it. It was my first local meeting as there was no IBA in Portland while I was there.

She had a second meeting and then she just disappeared off the face of the earth. Shortly after that I received a call from Howard Zieden at GKIC about becoming the Austin IBA. Carol and I had decided to move to Phoenix where we have children and grandchildren so I told Howard I would not be interested and why. A few weeks later, Howard called again to inform me that the Phoenix East chapter would be available by the end of the summer.

I flew to Phoenix and met with the "resigning" IBA, Josh Beistle, to complete my due diligence. To me it seemed a "no brainer." I would be hitched to the heavy wagon of my marketing idol, Dan Kennedy. I would also be in position to expand my current life's purpose to use my experience and talent to help businesses to succeed.

Soon I was in Cleveland with some other new IBA's and prospective IBA's for indoctrination and training (GKIC called it a Discovery Day). I learned that Discovery Days were a very sound strategy for group selling.

In August of 2008 I held my first GKIC Chapter Meeting. Only I did not put it on. I attended as a prospective member to learn the lay of the land. Dr. Ron Marek was conducting the meetings for Josh so I paid him to put on a meeting for me. He did a great job, but there were only 13 people in attendance.

I called 30 members at random who were not in attendance. Of the 30, 22 either took my call or returned my call. The response was overwhelming – change the time of day and location of the meetings. That was easy to fix.

> ★ **BIG LESSON**
>
> Pick up the phone! Don't hide behind email. I've already explained why I don't trust surveys and focus groups.

Howard Zieden warned me not launch a Mastermind Group until I had been an IBA for a while. I ignored the advice because I had belonged to Mastermind groups and facili-tated them for many years.

We launched the first Phoenix Mastermind Group with a Discovery Day in December of 2008 and held our first Mas-termind Meeting in January of 2009. We started with seven members. I'm very proud to say that three of the original members, Zach Wilsterman, Rich Rose and Victor Allison, have been continuous members for 3 ½ years as of this writing.

I'm biased of course, but I know of no other activity that assists entrepreneurs in accelerating both their business growth and personal growth than belonging to a Mastermind group of like- minded people.

There are two types of Mastermind Groups – industry specific and "mixed breed." I was in industry specific Masterminds in both the auto parts industry and the golf industry. In "mixed breed" groups all the members are from different industries. To me these are by far the best to belong to if you're only going to belong to one Mastermind Group. If you belong to multiple groups then you may select an industry specific group, too.

The Mastermind principle is discussed in depth in Napoleon Hill's book, *Think and Grow Rich.* Andrew Carnegie, Henry Ford, Thomas Edison, Harvey Firestone, and other industrial icons of the time credit their Mastermind group as a principle reason for their success and wealth. Carnegie said the strength of ten minds working on a business was not one mind multiplied by ten but of one mind multiplied by 100. Very powerful stuff.

A very interesting phenomenon about participating in a Mastermind group is that you get as much out of working on someone else's business as you do when the group works on your business. I've seen it in my businesses and seen it in others time and time again. You are actively participating with your group and dispensing advice when shazam! You pick up a great idea that you can use that's worth thousands of dollars to you.

Currently I'm facilitating three Mastermind groups in the Phoenix area which meet monthly and one national group which meets three times a year in a different location each time.

> **Opportunity:** If you truly want to up your game, contact my office at 480-773-7490 to see if seats are available and if you qualify.

I also pay to belong to two Mastermind groups. I don't believe one should facilitate a group without also belonging to an outside group. Coaches need coaches, too.

CHAPTER 16

Private Clients

There's a saying around GKIC said sarcastically, "But my business is different." I was in that rut at one time myself. But the truth is we're not all that different. Good marketing is essential for all businesses to prosper as are fundamental business practices. You have to know ALL your numbers whether you run an auto parts distribution company, golf stores, a law practice, dental practice, etc.

In the interest of maintaining confidentiality of my clients I won't use names or businesses here, but I will list the categories of businesses I've worked with. And let me say it has been a true blessing to work with each and every one of them.

Previously I mentioned that I got started in consulting by working with an auto parts store and golf equipment store. I've also worked with professionals in the following business types:

- Landscape design
- Women's clothing stores
- Law

- Accounting
- Residential real estate
- Commercial real estate
- Marketing strategy
- Consulting
- Business coaching
- Internet marketing (oxymoron because the internet is a media)
- Hypnotherapy
- Personal training
- Off-road vehicle manufacturing
- Machine shops
- Dentistry
- Hearing centers
- Credit restoration
- Financial planning
- Insurance

We have had some marvelous success stories and of course failures, also. It makes me so very proud of my clients and gives me such great pleasure when they say, "I'm having my best year ever." I've heard those beautiful words a number of times and I never will tire of hearing them.

There are three major frustrations in the consulting world:

The lessor of the three is that clients often select a consultant by price. The client ends up hiring someone who has never met a payroll, placed an ad, or sought financing in their life. When you've been there you add depth and the wisdom of experience to your recommendations.

A very frustrating occurrence for a consultant is imple-
mentation. Why would a business hire someone for their
expertise and experience, spend hours in planning, agree
with every suggestion and then do nothing? If you know
the answer, let me know!

And finally the biggie… a client or Mastermind member
has tremendous success. You as the consultant and / or
the Mastermind group gave them the ideas, confidence,
support and accountability they needed for their success.
They take all the credit with their employees, peers, and at
home which is fine. But… they believe their press clippings,
get the big head, and blow it with ego driven decisions
and living like they have the King Midas touch.

> ★ **BIG LESSON**
>
> There's a cliché that says your ego is your most costly
> possession. Believe that cliché and guard against it. If
> you're having great success, revel in it but remember
> what got you to it.

CHAPTER 17

Customer Service as a Marketing Tactic

I am an absolute customer service fanatic. I wrote an article and crafted a training seminar on customer service that is appropriate for a book about learning marketing lessons from the streets.

Dan Kennedy teaches that Disney categorizes their janitorial expenses at their theme parks as marketing expenses. I think that is brilliant.

Be an Absolute Customer Service Fanatic!

I'm from the old school and I believe you have to be an absolute fanatic about the customer service you offer your customers, clients, or patients. This means whether you have a retail business, wholesale business, internet business, accounting business, dental practice, medical practice, law firm, landscape business, construction company, or any other kind of business.

It does not matter! Be <u>freaky</u> about your attention to customer service. Every detail matters.

I will say it again (and again, and again, and again). It's the most important thing you can do – particularly in light of the new economy. You know people are cranky and they don't accept sub-standard customer service. They expect excellence and you had better provide it if you want to stay in business. And I've got some stories from my past businesses that are very interesting.

When I was in the retail golf business, I was always astonished at events that occurred because my managers were schooled on customer service, as were my employees.

First, I was always amazed at the condition of my store's parking lots. Just walking from where I parked my car to the door, depending on what store it was, there would be a handful of candy wrappers and in those days, when smoking was more prevalent, cigarette pack wrappers, cigarette butts, you name it.

Even packages from something someone bought in my store and tore open before they climbed into their car. I would come in the store and I'd throw the trash away and I'd say to the employees, "Gee, didn't anyone see this garbage when they came in here?" And I'd get these blank looks and they would say, "Well, that wasn't there when we came in." BS!

You and I both know it was on the ground when they came to work. They just walked from their car to their place of employment with blinders on and didn't see any of it.

But, I guarantee as a shopper, when I go to a store, I see that stuff and either consciously or unconsciously I make decisions about the establishment as I'm walking in. You do too. That first impression thing also applies to businesses as well as people you meet.

> ★ **BIG LESSON**
>
> When you and your employees walk into your business, you MUST see it from the eyes of your clients or patients. They are making decisions about you that may frighten you, if you don't do what I suggest.

I talked to the managers and the employees constantly about how, when we walk into our stores, we all had to feel like we were the customer. From the time you get out of the car until the time that you walk into the store, think like a customer.

This also applies if you have a medical or dental office. Visualize this. You're in a waiting room at a doctor's office or dentist's office and the room needs painting or the walls are dirty or there's "dust bunnies" on the floor. Do you kind of think behind the scenes, back where the patient rooms are, that they also might not be as clean as they should be? I know those thoughts go through my mind.

But every time you walk into your business, whether you're a retailer, a wholesaler, a doctor, a dentist, a veterinarian, an accountant, it doesn't matter. Walk into that business like you were the customer/patient with your eyes wide open. That's the perfect time for you NOT to be thinking about what you have going on that day. Think like you are your customer.

I have spoken to previous medical care providers about these kinds of things. Note I said previous because they did not clean and paint. Apparently they are like my retail employees were and didn't see it from the patient's eyes.

My wife had a former cardiologist like this. His finger nails were in bad need of a manicure. His office looked like it was out of the 1950s and probably had not been painted since then either. His bedside manner also sucked. This doctor could probably double his business if he gave any thought to the patients' experience when they had an appointment with him.

If your parking lot is cracked or the lines need to be repainted, it is probably a landlord's problem for most businesses. You pay for the maintenance of those things in your common area maintenance charges so you should be complaining about them. If the parking lot looks like crap then complain every day until it gets repaired.

It's one of those visual things that your customers may never say anything about, but believe me – <u>they notice</u>.

Do you have background music in your business? If you do, you have to be very careful about WHAT KIND of music is in the background. What is the safest music to play for your KEY demographic of customer? If your best customers are people 50 and up, do you allow your employees to listen to rap because that is what they like? I surely hope not!

Customer Service Pet Peeves

I have several pet peeves on customer service and since I am a fanatic, I want to share them. Some of these are nit-picky and some of them are just common sense things.

You must hire mystery shoppers. When you hire mystery shoppers, set up the shopping scenario for exactly what you are concerned about, because you could be measuring the employee's:

- Product knowledge
- Sales language
- Attire
- Attitude
- Attentiveness

- Greeting: was it warm?

- Smile: do they smile?

And by the way, mystery shoppers are not just for retailers. They should also be used in business to business commerce, medical practices, and ANY business that has customer or prospect contact over the phone, or on the internet. Not just in person.

You should also have people call and ask for things. It may be something as simple as making an appointment at your dental office. Does the person who answers the phone, answer the phone quickly? Are they business-like but friendly when they answer the phone? Are they chewing gum? Are they using slang expressions that would appall you if you were a dentist and your average patient pays you $1,500/year?

If you call in to your business yourself, all you're going to hear is the employees give their greeting, which should be scripted. As soon as they know it's you, everything will change. So hire a mystery shopping service or have a friend call in, but have those conversations recorded so you can play them back.

> ### ★ BIG LESSON
>
> You will get a great return on the investment you make in mystery shopping. It is the only true way to know if your customer service policies are followed.

Recently I had my first appointment with a new urologist. The office was modern and furnished nicely. The waiting room was clean. When I was brought into the treatment area I was taken to the doctor's office, not a treatment room.

Initially I think this is a nice touch. But as I sit, waiting for him, I notice his office is more cluttered than my home office. There are papers, files, and binders stacked everywhere. That's OK if you aren't going to have customers, clients, or patients meeting in your office.

When my appointment was over I was sent to the check-out desk. The young woman at the desk was talking to another patient on the phone. The other patient was obviously irate. She put the irate patient on hold and talked to another staff member on the intercom in a derogatory manner about the person on hold.

She never should have been answering the phone where I or any other patients could hear the dirty laundry being aired. Then, when she talked to me, she yawned literally at least 12 times. Horrible etiquette.

Sloppy desk and untrained staff – does that mean sloppy urologist? I don't know but just the thought crossing my mind is not good for that urology practice.

Another Pet Peeve

You walk into a store and the person that is supposed to be waiting on you is on their cell phone and it takes four or five minutes for them to end their call. You can just sense this is a personal call, particularly because it's on the cell phone. So you're standing there on one foot and then the other. Now do you feel like giving that place your hard earned money? I think not.

See and hear everything as you walk through your office. The mystery shopper will shed some light on this. But are your employees doing personal e-mails on your time? Are they surfing the web on your time? Are they texting friends on your time? Are they making personal phone calls on your time?

I think that every business could save a minimum of 10 percent off their payroll if they could control what I call time theft, where you're actually paying your employees to be doing something else. Now I know some of you that hire younger people say, "Well, everyone expects to be able to do those things." And I say, "why?" If you're paying someone for an hour's worth of work why should they spend 15 or 20 minutes of that time doing personal things? If they want to work someplace else, let them, it's OK. Sometimes you have to do some cutting or cleaving, as I call it, to get down to the right staff for your needs.

Another Retail Example

I walk into a hardware store and I need some help finding an item. But the clerk is on his cell phone texting. What's my immediate thought? My immediate thought is that I'm not as important to this business as I should be. I don't want to spend my money here. If the employee spends a lot of time behind their computer screen, without recognizing me, I assume they are on the internet. Next time I will probably go to a competitor. There are plenty of hardware stores.

> ★ **BIG LESSON**
>
> If your staff is ignoring your customers or patients to complete a personal call or text, you have a problem. Your sales are slumping or not increasing. You MUST limit personal communications while on duty.

Hey Buddy, How About That Slang?

Something else you need to do is to develop the ability to hear everything. We have some slang used now in our society that can be offensive depending on the age and or gender of your clients.

Recently I walked into an automotive shop in Phoenix to get

a quote on some air conditioning work. The first thing out of the mouth of the employee who greeted me was, "Hi buddy, be with you in a minute."

The "hi buddy" gets me. I'm not his buddy and I'm not his pal. If I was a woman I wouldn't be his darlin' or his little lady. I was a potential customer coming into an auto repair shop.

This continues throughout the whole conversation. "Well, buddy, what year is that car?… Really, and why do you think that work needs to done, buddy?… Buddy, we can get that done for you right away. Can I schedule that for you, buddy?" At that point, I am walking out. It is not the place that I want to be.

I'm not his friend. My friends may call me buddy or pal, but most of the time they would say, "Hi Chuck" as opposed to "hi buddy" or "hi pal."

I got the air conditioning repair done at Hi-Tech Car Care in Phoenix. The customer service was superb! It was my first time in the shop. I was greeted immediately. I was spoken to as Mr. Trautman until I said just call me "Chuck." I was asked to fill out a form that not only asked for my basic personal and vehicle information, but ask for my preferences in coffee, tea, soft drinks, newspapers, magazines, and more.

The waiting room was clean and stocked with two local newspapers, USA Today, Wall Street Journal, many magazine titles, bottled water, both regular and decaf coffee, and assorted soft drinks – in a refrigerator not a vending machine.

The shop owner, James Garnand, obviously has designed a customer experience and trained his people on how to deliver the experience.

Compare that experience to "Hi Buddy"?

Another thing that troubles me in customer service is when someone does something for you which is part of their job and we thank them. Since most of us are courteous people when someone brings us a glass of water in a restaurant, we say, "Thank you." Then the server says, "No problem." Well, of course it was no problem, it was their job. What is wrong with, "You're welcome?"

> ★ **BIG LESSON**
>
> Your employees don't even realize they are offending your clients with their "hip" dialog. Train them to be mindful of how they speak to older clients and clients of the opposite gender.

Chick-fil-A is an example of a company who has trained their people very, very well. Their staff says, "You're welcome" or better yet, most of the time they say, "My pleasure" when you thank them for serving you.

Recently I ate lunch at the Applebee's at 44th and Thomas in Phoenix. It was a great experience. When I walked into the Applebee's the young "host" seated us, and asked, "Can I get you something to drink?" I replied, "Yes, some ice water, please." When he brought the ice water back, I said, "Thank you" and he said, "Well, it was my pleasure, sir, thank you for coming in."

What a breath of fresh air! Later in the luncheon, the manager came over and wanted to know how the customer service had been. And since I had enjoyed excellent customer service from the waitress as well, I told him it was excellent. He said some classic words which I thought were perfect, "I'm really glad to hear that. That means my training is paying off." How important is training? Well, it's incredibly important and should be a big part of your life.

Empower Your Employees

Empower your employees to make decisions. I always go by the golden rule business philosophy. And this is not a religious statement whatsoever. It's just that if we treat our customers, our employees and our suppliers exactly the way we like to be treated, we can't go wrong.

I feel the same way about employees working for us. Whether they are a receptionist or hygienist in the dentist's office, the nurse in the doctor's office, or a retail employee, it does not matter. If they are trained and empowered to treat your customers, patients or your clients exactly the same way that they would want to be treated, they will make good decisions.

In my golf stores, I had a policy that the second time I heard an employee say "according to company policy", I would fire them. That's a strong statement, but how do you feel when someone hides behind "according to company policy"? I mean, who sets these policies? There's an exception to every policy.

We could go on and on, but those are words that will make your customers, patients and clients bristle. So NEVER allow the phrase "according to company policy" be uttered to a customer or client in your business.

> ★ **BIG LESSON**
>
> Institute a "Golden Rule" business philosophy in your business today. You won't be sorry.

Handling Money

More pet peeves that need to be addressed - How can we struggle with the simple counting back of change? With computers, counting back change has become a lost art.

Why have a bill for $64.47, fork over $70 and have someone put the change in your hand? At least the employee could hand over the coin and say, "65 and 5 makes 70." It doesn't happen anymore. At the least they can say your change is $5.53 and hand it back to you and not just hand you the money and expect you count it out.

And another biggie on the handling of money, is <u>how</u> you get change back. Say you buy something that costs $2. You get handed back $18 in change and some of the bills have the heads up, some of them have the heads down, some of them have the heads facing left, some of them have them facing right, because that's the way they pulled them out of the cash drawer.

Now, it may be anal, but my employees were required to keep the drawer straight, meaning all the heads were up and all the heads were facing one way or the other. They were required to hand back change with the heads up and all facing the same way.

My preference is to have the heads facing left but it doesn't really matter. What is important is put the money back in the customer's hands neatly. Whenever my staff received money from the customer, if it was handed to them upside down and heads facing different directions, they simply sorted it as they put it in the drawer. So when we pulled our cash drawers down at night to make our bank deposit, our money was always orderly. I think it's a sign of sloppiness when the money comes back wadded up.

Phones

I've mentioned this before but when the phone is the life blood of your business, you need to have a script as to exactly how you want your phones answered. Whether you want them to use, "Good morning," "Good afternoon," or whether you want them to say, "Doctor's offices" or "Law Offices" and use their name, it is important the phone be answered the same by every employee. Teach your staff at all times to answer the phone with a smile on their face so the customer on the other end of the phone hears a smile.

And the phone voice cannot be quick. "Joe's Auto Parts" can be said real fast where the words are all run together or it can be, "Joe's AUTO Parts" so that the person knows exactly who they're talking to.

My first business, Harr Motor Supply, was an auto parts store in Eugene, OR. It was mainly a wholesale store. Service stations, garages and fleets called in orders and we delivered them. My guys would answer the phones so fast it was amazing. It was OK for those wholesale customers because they knew who they were calling and recognized the employee from his voice.

But 20 percent of our business was retail. I just knew the retail customer was asking the salesperson, "What did you say?" or "Who's this?" because they couldn't tell they'd actually reached Harr Motor Supply and they thought they had dialed a wrong number.

If you want the name of your business mentioned, which you should, it should be said slowly, clearly, with enthusiasm and with a smile. Your staff should say their first name, too.

My golf stores were named International Golf. We would say, "Good morning, International Golf, Chuck speaking" and then the client on the phone would often pick up our names and be friendly. It helps develop rapport which is part of the sales strategy.

Another big item to consider in using the phone in retail environments is you have to talk to your employees and your managers about the value of the money in hand versus the money to come on the phone. It's a very delicate thing.

Let's say I'm standing in a hardware store. The cashier is ringing up my purchase on a plumbing item. They get interrupted by a phone call. If I have to stand around for four or five minutes because they take the phone call, I become very annoyed. I'm sure you do too.

Money in hand versus the phone call – which is best? There needs to be a system in place if someone has to talk to you when you're in the act of waiting on a customer. Your employee can take a message, or you can get on the phone and say, "Let me get your telephone number, I'll call you right back, I'm with a customer." Make it a very, very quick interruption and be sure to apologize to the person in front of you. The interruptions are bound to happen but we need to know how to handle them when they do.

Answering Machine Messages

Too many options makes for confused customers, clients, and patients. A classic at doctor's offices is (after we get by "press #1 for English and press #2 for Spanish"), "Call 911 if this is an emergency, press #1 if you are another doctor, press #2 for records, press #3 to leave a message for the doctor or nurse, press #4 to make an appointment, or press #0 to talk to the receptionist."

It is too long. By the time they get through the list I have to listen a second time and by then I am pissed!

★ BIG LESSON

Your phone is often your business's first contact with a customer or prospect. Treat it with reverence! Use mystery shoppers to insure your phone scripts are being followed.

Customer Service for Immediate Sales

Here are some terrific customer service tips I've used to increase sales immediately. They were very, very effective in both my auto parts stores and my retail golf equipment stores.

One was to match the coupons or sale prices of our competitors. This is a big deal because it's worth a lot to you in sales and it is also a solid customer service function.

One of my golf stores in Portland, OR was on 82nd Avenue and was two blocks away from a Nevada Bob's golf store. We both, of course, ran different kinds of advertising and people would sometimes get confused about which store they were going to. They might see my store because it was not in a shopping center, like Nevada Bob's. It was a free standing building. Often customers thought they were going to Nevada Bob's to respond to their ad, but in fact came to my store.

So my sales staff was taught that if someone came in and said "yes, I've come in to pick up those golf balls on sale", we sold them to them even though we were not advertising that brand at the time.

We cut copies of Nevada Bob's and any other competitor's ads out of the newspapers or out of their direct mail pieces. We also cut out their coupons and kept them in our store. We would simply match the price. We would go so far as to put "As Advertised" signs on items THEY were advertising.

If they had a deal on Spalding golf balls on a weekend sale at $9.97 per 15-ball pack and someone came in looking for the $9.97 golf balls, you better believe we sold them the golf ball at $9.97 because we didn't want that customer going up the street. We wanted them to establish the habit to coming to our store for all their golf equipment and accessory needs.

Another thing we did, both in auto parts and golf, was to call other stores in the area. For instance, the customer is looking for a water pump for a '94 Chevrolet and we're out of stock on the item. Rather than say, "Sorry, we don't have it," we would say, "Sir, I don't have that in stock right now, I can get that for you from my warehouse or can I call around for you?"

> ### ★ BIG LESSON
>
> This is a big customer service tip that keeps your customers coming back forever. They sincerely appreciate the time you have saved them. Your other major benefit is you get the opportunity to make the related sales.

We would also call manufacturers in the golf business or our warehouse distributors in the auto parts business to check on items we did not have in stock. And even though we wanted the customer back in the store to pick the item up when it came in, because they might buy something else, we always offered to ship it at our expense to their home or office.

Now think about that for a minute. You've come in to my store to buy the latest TaylorMade driver. And you need to have it in a 9 degree loft with a stiff shaft. And I'm out of stock on it. I say, "I'm out of stock on that but I'll have TaylorMade ship one directly to your house and I'll pay the freight." Now, what are you thinking? *"Wow, I don't have to run around and find this thing and I don't even have to pay the freight, it will come directly from the factory."* Now, of course, we took the money at the time of the sale but that money stayed in our store instead of the customer going to another golf store to buy it.

In auto parts it also was a big deal to our customer. You're going to put new brakes on your car on the weekend and it's

Wednesday. We don't have the wheel cylinder kits that you needed in stock.

Rather than have you go to another store, and maybe get all the brake parts, we sell you the disc brake pads, brake shoes and the hardware. Since we don't have the rear wheel cylinder kits in stock, we ship them at our expense from our warehouse distributor to your home or office. Or, we pick them up at our warehouse distributor and ship them out of our store to your home or office. But the bottom line is we've kept the money in our business and kept that customer satisfied so he's not going out and possibly experiencing a competitor's great customer service.

One of my mentors, Dan Kennedy, calls this building "an iron cage around your herd" – doing anything that you can to keep your customer with you instead of sending them someplace else. Don't give them the chance to experience somebody else's service. They don't want to, because your service is so good. Visualize your customers being a herd and you have a fence around them so that they are always your customer.

Building Your List

Earlier we discussed list building and contact with your customers in detail. However from a customer service standpoint it is very important to communicate with your customers on a regular basis.

In my golf stores, way before it was fashionable and before e-mail and computers were as a big as they are now, I used to pay a spiff or a commission to my sales staff to gather the customer contact information from our customer or our prospect.

We would simply say "we have a golf tips newsletter, if you'd like to find out about the most recent golf tips, or the most recent equipment coming out, please give us your name and address or name and e-mail address, and we'll get you on our list." I would pay twenty five cents a name in commission to build the list. Otherwise the employees would not consistently ask for the information.

Sometimes I would pay fifty cents if I wanted to make it a real big deal to make sure everybody got in the habit of asking for the contact information. I would say I'm going to pay fifty cents for every new name that you guys get. I had a person on my staff that entered the names into "Constant Contact", which I was using at the time for the e-mail side of it. They would enter the info into Excel spreadsheets for our hard copy newsletter.

> ★ **BIG LESSON**
>
> Be an absolute customer service fanatic. Make sure your employees know you are <u>dedicated</u> to providing long term, excellent customer experiences.

The next example comes from the auto parts distribution business. Our customers were all wholesale customers. We owned a few auto parts stores of our own, but our distribution center customers were wholesale customers. They were automotive parts stores who were buying parts from us for resale.

We received their regular stock orders daily. We had delivery trucks which delivered to our customers every night after business hours. Our delivery routes were all over western and central Oregon, up into Chehalis and Centralia in Washington, and down into Yreka and Crescent City in Northern California.

In addition to stock orders going out every night, there would be special orders, which were critical. Imagine this. You were driving from San Francisco to Portland, Oregon and you had a part fail on your car in Yreka, CA and it was not a common part. None of the stores or car dealers in Yreka had the part you needed. You could not get your car repaired until a part arrived so you were going to be stuck there.

Here's how we came into the picture. If an auto parts store in that town got an order in for your part by 5 PM, it would be in their store at 8 AM the next morning. These trucks delivered overnight. This was a tremendous service for the consumer, who was having the part installed by a professional installer because they weren't marooned for two or three days in some obscure little town.

It was also a hell of a good service for our auto parts store customers to pass on to their customers. Think about ways that you can go "outside the box" to provide exceptional service.

My Ramada Inn Story

Speaking of my Carquest days reminds me of another story. This is no slam on the Ramada Inn chain because I have enjoyed many good experiences at Ramada Inns over the years, but this story is too good not to tell.

In the early days of my Carquest business, the early 1980s, we had offices in both Portland and Eugene. I lived in Eugene at the time. There was a nice Ramada Inn in Tualatin, Oregon a couple of miles from our Portland distribution center. I stayed there when I worked out of the Portland office. Many reps, from both automotive and other industries stayed there, as well.

One night after a few cocktails I went to the restaurant for a late night breakfast with a couple of friends. That was the norm in the 80s. Although the sign said, "Please wait to be seated," there was no one to seat us, so after waiting a few minutes we found an empty table and seated ourselves. The place was almost full which was unusual for that time of night.

After a 15-minute wait, we still had not spoken to a waitress or waiter. So I got up went behind the counter and got us three glasses of water and brought the coffee pot back to our table and poured us coffee.

Other customers now thought I worked there and asked for refills. I obliged by walking around the restaurant topping off coffee and filling water glasses. None of the staff who was working questioned me about who I was or what I was doing.

By now I was having fun with it. My friends were hysterical, so I continued entertaining them by seating customers as they arrived and getting them water and coffee.

Food orders were not being placed for some of the customers so I found an order pad behind the counter, took orders, and turned them in to the kitchen. Still nobody working said a thing to me. I guess they all thought I was the "new guy." I wonder what they and the customers thought about the alcohol on my breath?

Finally a lady appears who obviously was the cashier/hostess. I was sure she would question me, but no. About 45 minutes into this gig some of my "customers" wanted their checks. So I got a menu, filled out the check with the correct prices and left it on their tables. Sure enough, they left me tips and paid the cashier.

By now I was tired of the game and left. In case you are wondering, I left the tips on the tables.

Two weeks later I had a guaranteed reservation for one night at the same hotel. I arrived about 11:30 PM. When I walked into the lobby, there was no one behind the check-in desk. After about five minutes I was pissed off.

In those days there were no key cards like what are used today. There were real keys. The keys were kept in little square boxes. If the key was in the box the room was vacant. So after waiting another five minutes, I took a key for an empty room and spent the night.

The next morning, when I got to my office, I called the hotel and told them that no one was behind the desk when I checked in so I stayed elsewhere. I instructed them not to charge my credit card for the guaranteed reservation. The clerk agreed.

Next I called back and spoke to the manager. He did not believe that I actually helped myself to a room. Then I told him about "working" in his restaurant. He did not believe that either. He thought I was a prankster of some kind. That was my last night at the Ramada. A short time later they sold out, remodeled the place, and turned it into a nice property, The Nyberg Inn. Now the property is a strip mall.

The lessons here are many fold. First of all I personally spent about 50 nights there before the last incident. Counting my employees, customers, and meeting space we spent at least 200 nights there and spent thousands of dollars on meeting rooms and catering. The manager should have known who I was and called me to schmooze long before the "incidents" just to say "thank you" and to establish a relationship.

> ★ **BIG LESSON**
>
> If you don't know your larger clients, give them a call and introduce yourself!

Secondly, you have got to check out negative reports about your staff. Think about the security issues. I probably could have cleaned out the cash register in the restaurant if I was dishonest. Someone had to be in charge – or was there? How could any staff member just let someone work who they had never seen before?

Anybody could have pulled their own key and spent the night in a hotel room for free. How about the safety of the other guests? How about the impression of the next guest who uses the room? It certainly would not have been on the "to be cleaned" list for the housekeeping staff.

> ★ **BIG LESSON**
>
> You have to have a relationship with your good customers. It's great to "defend" your employees. But if you get an outlandish complaint, check it out – it's probably true.

Dealing With Angry Customers

Let's face it, even when we've improved our customer service to "great", we are going to piss off some people. How you deal with the angry customer is a key to keeping them.

Provide your staff training on dealing with irate customers, because mistakes do happen. You can turn that irate customer into a long term customer if you use the proper techniques.

First of all, when someone is angry, don't step on their words. Don't talk over the top of them. Be sure to let them vent, let them get it all out. Accept responsibility for the mistake and tell them you're going to do everything you can to rectify it. The worst thing you can do is be argumentative. I've seen it happen and talked to employees and managers and even disciplined them, because they get confrontational with an angry customer or client. You're never going to win that one so why try? The person came in mad and they are going to stay mad unless you let them talk it out.

It is very, very important to let your employees know that when someone comes in mad, find out what the problem is but don't interrupt. Don't talk over the top of them. They might go on a rant for 45 seconds, but eventually they've got it all out and then you calmly need to say, "Well, Mr. Jones, I can certainly understand why you're angry. If that happened to me, I would be angry too, so let's figure out the best way for us to deal with this." And then legitimately figure out a solution.

Remember the golden rule business philosophy? Treat your angry customer the way you would want to be treated if it was you who was upset with a business you were trading at. If it's a refund issue, give the refund cheerfully. If a replacement is required, give the replacement cheerfully. Whatever it takes to satisfy and control the situation. Again, it's that golden rule business philosophy, your employee needs to deal with that person exactly the way that they would want to be dealt with if the roles were reversed.

Take the golf business. Someone was sold a club with the wrong shaft. They were fit for a regular shaft and walked out of the store with a firm shaft. Frankly, the customer could have been fit in our hitting cages and then gone back to the rack and pulled the wrong one himself. Our person at the counter doesn't recognize what's happened and goes ahead and rings up the club with the wrong shaft. Now the golfer plays his first round with the new club and doesn't hit the club well because the shaft is too stiff for him.

It was that customer's fault to some degree, but mostly it was our fault. So even though the club is now a used club, and we have to sell it for less money, we of course exchanged it for the proper club.

In the auto parts distribution business we double checked all outgoing special orders to prevent shipping the wrong part. Even then we occasionally screwed up an order. On more than one occasion I jumped in my car and drove four hours round trip to appease and bail out a large customer.

Could I have sent someone else? Sure I could have, but imagine the statement I made to my customer – that the owner of a $25 million business would personally fix the mistake. I built and cemented some great relationships and built that "iron cage around my herd."

Gift Returns

This is an area where you can capture a customer for life or lose one for life. People often try to return gifts and they don't have a receipt. It's a judgment call to do what is best depending on the situation. But remember you NEVER say, "According to company policy." Use the golden rule so you arrive at what is best to either create a long term customer or keep a situation from escalating into being out of hand.

In the big box retail world it is very popular to give gift cards instead of refunds if the customer wants to return something they don't have a receipt for or it was too many days since the sale, etc.

That's fine, unless your customer objects, and then you need to do something about it. I can remember a personal incident where I purchased a Sirius radio for my wife for a birthday gift and also purchased an in-home version. I wasn't sure whether we would use the in-home version or not but the salesman said, "Oh, it'd be OK, no problem with the return."

Her birthday came, she got the gift, we found out the same Sirius channels were available on our cable television package so we had no need for the home version. I called to make an appointment for installation for the car, and long story short, by the time the installation was made we were past Best Buy's 30-day limit for getting your cash back.

The radio was going in a SL 320 Mercedes and the installers had trouble mounting the receiver and mounting the radio, so I had to come back which put us past 30 days. So I have the problem of them wanting to give me a gift card for $175 or $180 because I was past the Best Buy policy limit.

I tried to explain the situation but of course, it was, "according to company policy." I was directed over to a separate desk and a young woman gave me the same, "according to company policy routine." I asked if I could speak to the manager of the store. She said she was the manager. I said, "No, no, not of this department, I want to speak to the manager of this particular Best Buy location." And she said, "Well, I am the manager." I said, "I do not believe that for one second. I demand to speak to the store general manager."

Miraculously, all of a sudden, she could discuss giving me my credit. By this time, I am irate, I am getting talked over the top of, talked down to, and generally being treated like I'm an idiot.

My fall-back position was, "Look, I purchased this on a credit card and I will contest this charge with my credit card company if I do not get a credit back immediately."

So very frumpily, angrily and with lots of negative emotion, she gave me my credit. It shouldn't have ever had to go that far. I had explained my situation, why it took more than 30 days, so there shouldn't have been any issue. Even though that was their policy, obviously she had the ability to override their policy because she eventually did. Think about this when dealing with your clients.

It was literally years before I bought anything from Best Buy again. I've also told this story at seminars, articles and now in a book.

> ★ **BIG LESSON**
>
> No one ever really wins an argument so why would you argue with a client. Resolve the issue the way you would want it resolved if you were the client.

The last (as a fanatic it is probably not the last!) thing I'm going to say about customer service is that a lot of times, we as business people, no matter whether we are retailers, distributors, installers, doctors, dentists, lawyers, accountants, tend to let operations drive decisions we make about sales and customer service instead of the other way. This is a critical mistake!

If you have a great marketing or sales idea or one of your key people do, and operationally someone says we can't do that because of this, that or the other thing, stop them quickly and ask them to figure out a way. In a very small percentage of the time, it is possible that something operationally will prevent you from doing what you want to do. But the last thing you want to do is to kill good sales potential and good customer service by letting operations dictate to you.

My policy has always been to figure out a way to make great marketing and sales ideas work – whatever it takes.

Internet Marketing and Customer Service

First of all the term "internet marketing" is an oxymoron. The internet is just a media, like newspapers, radio, email, etc.

Great customer service is just as important if you sell only on the internet. Maybe even more important because your customer never sees you.

Think about your customer in the lowest common denominator. They might not be computer savvy, so everything you do needs to be simple and customer friendly. If you have something for them to do, like download a program to watch a video or download a PDF, then spell out the instructions clearly so they will do what they need to do.

It will save you returns and it will save your customer frustration. They will keep coming back to your site to shop again and again.

Your websites need to be very customer friendly. Don't think about the techies, unless you're in the technical business, but worry about the lowest common denominator of customer.

It could be an older person who doesn't have a lot of computer savvy, or has an older computer which doesn't have a lot of memory. Think about these things. Keep it as SIMPLE as you can and give detailed instructions.

Everything else we discussed in this section also applies to your internet business. Have your address and phone number displayed prominently. Too many sites make contacting the business next to impossible.

Use a mystery shopper for your internet site. Ask someone to buy something from your site, contact the site for customer service, watch the follow up communication, and return the item for credit. Their honest feedback may be very valuable to you.

If you incorporate these tips and strategies into your business you will gain more sales, have less returns, and be more profitable – guaranteed!

CONCLUSION

Are you an avid reader? If not, become one! Dan Kennedy tells a story about being in the green room with Donald Trump. Trump asked what THREE books he was currently reading because Trump did not want to miss a book that might help him.

I read 35 to 45 books a year. I love it, but also it keeps me sharp and abreast of current trends and gives me fresh ideas. I also listen to about 150 hours of recorded interviews with experts a year and attend three to five national marketing events annually. It contributes to my knowledge and allows me to bring incredible value to my clients.

I've really enjoyed writing this book. Use these tips and stories to improve your sales and profits.

Made in the USA
Charleston, SC
05 January 2013